The Australian Women's Weekly cookbooks

Brigid Treloar

In association with *The Australian Women's Weekly* Test Kitchen

Although sushi is a great favourite in our household, I didn't know much about Japanese food until we started this book. Now, teppanyaki is at the top of my favourites list – a combination of marinated ingredients that cook in minutes and everyone helps themselves (see page 100). It's the type of family meal I'm always looking for – quick, healthy and delicious – like most of the recipes in the book, as it turns out. Give it a try – this could be the start of your love affair with Japanese food.

Pamela Clark

Food Editor

contents

tasting japan

From Sydney to San Francisco and London, you can hardly walk a block in almost any city centre without passing a noodle bar or sushi shop.

Japanese food is enormously satisfying on many levels – not only is it delicious but it is also low in fat, deceptively simple to prepare, beautiful in its presentation and healthy, using only the freshest of all seasonal produce.

The Japanese are well known for their trim figures and longevity, and this is largely attributed to their diet. Their cooking methods – boiling, grilling, baking, barbecuing, steaming and simmering in broth – have very little added fat, include no heavy sauces and make use of subtle seasonings to enhance the food's natural flavour.

At first, some Japanese food may seem bland, and it may take a bit of time and experimentation to develop a real appreciation for it. Much emphasis is placed on the freshness and quality of the raw produce, the treatment of it, from preparation through to garnish, and presentation at the table. The Japanese believe that food should look as good as it tastes, that it should appeal to all senses.

The main ingredients in the Japanese kitchen are rice, the freshest fish, a wide variety of vegetables and soy bean products (tofu, miso, soy sauce) – all foods that we know to be of importance for a healthy diet. **Rice** is a basic source of carbohydrate and protein, **fish** is important for omega-3 fatty acids and vitamin B12, **fresh vegetables** for their excellent supply of vitamins, minerals, anti-oxidants and fibre, and **soy beans** (in tofu, soy sauce and miso) are high in protein, iron and minerals. **Nori**, the seaweed used in wrapped sushi, is also rich in vitamins and minerals, especially iodine, and even the sinus-clearing, hot **wasabi** (japanese horseradish) is rich in vitamin C.

A Japanese meal almost always includes rice and, as a rule, the dishes are served all at once rather than in courses. Small portions are taken from each dish at random. Anything not liked can be left on the plate but it is considered bad manners to leave any rice, which is held in high regard because it has been the main food of the Japanese people for centuries. Although a Japanese meal traditionally consists of many small courses with small servings, quantities can easily be adjusted for a more Western-style main course meal.

Plan the meal using meat, fish and vegetables, and each dish using a different cooking method, such as grilled, steamed and fried. Remember always to select ingredients that are in season – yes, even seafood – both so your meal reflects the time of year and because it will be more economical. Not all ingredients listed in a recipe have to be used: mix and match according to the market and your individual taste and budget.

Every Japanese meal, including breakfast, traditionally includes at least one soup and rice. Even the simplest meal consists of soup, rice, pickles and green tea. Green tea is usually served at the beginning and throughout the meal.

do's and don'ts of japanese etiquette

■ When giving or receiving food, it is polite to use both hands to lift the bowl.

■ If using new disposable wooden or bamboo chopsticks, split them apart and scrape one against the other to remove any splinters.

■ Never stick chopsticks into food. The tips of chopsticks should not touch the table, so always use chopstick rests or the side of the plate. Rests can be as simple as a folded napkin or even the folded paper sleeve from the chopsticks.

■ Use your own chopsticks to take food from a communal dish if no serving implements are provided, but turn them around and use the clean handle end. Turn right way around again to use them for picking up your own food.

■ Japanese plates rarely match like a Western dinner service. Plates are chosen for colour, shape and texture to complement the food served. Plates, bowls, dipping bowls and even sake cups should never be filled to capacity; it is considered bad manners.

■ It is acceptable practice to slurp hot tea, soup and noodles both as a sign of enjoyment and to cool the liquid.

■ Since the dishes that make the meal are all served at once, you can take individual portions from any particular dish you wish, in whatever order you prefer.

■ To begin, remove the lid of your rice bowl and place it upside down so it doesn't drip onto the table. Do the same with your soup bowl. If the lid sticks because of the vacuum created inside, gently squeeze the sides of the bowl to release the lid.

■ Bowls of rice can be lifted to your mouth, to help you eat it more efficiently using chopsticks.

■ It is quite acceptable to eat sushi with your fingers. In Japan, sushi is sometimes served without chopsticks since it's assumed that only the fingers will be used.

■ If eaten with your fingers, nigiri-zushi (raw fish draped over a small hand-formed ball of rice) is eaten upside down so the sauce-dipped fish comes into contact with your tastebuds first, followed by the seasoned rice. If eating with chopsticks, turn nigiri-zushi on its side to dip fish into soy sauce. If the rice ball is dipped in the sauce, it falls apart.

■ When serving sashimi with soy sauce and wasabi on the side, it is traditional to serve the wasabi and soy sauce separately, that is, not to mix the ingredients. This is because the wasabi does nothing to enhance either the flavour or sensation of the sauce. Eat pink pickled ginger (gari) or shredded daikon to cleanse the palate between mouthfuls.

■ Sake is to the Japanese as wine is to the French. There are different sakes, sweet or dry, of different grades, that can be drunk warmed (40°C to 50°C) or chilled.

■ The sake cup must always be lifted when being filled from the sake bottle.

■ You should never pour your own drinks. Offer to serve others and wait for someone to offer to fill your cup; if someone fills your cup, reciprocate. Don't overfill the cup or glass. An empty glass or cup means you would like a refill. If you don't want any more, leave it full.

■ Wring out thin moistened wash-cloths or tiny hand-towels, roll tightly, then heat in the microwave oven briefly to offer at the beginning and end of the meal for guests to wipe their hands and refresh themselves.

glossary

bamboo mat *makisua*
large or small mat made from bamboo sticks tied together with cotton string, essential when preparing rolled sushi (maki-zushi); after use, wash well with scrubbing brush. Stand on end to dry thoroughly to avoid it becoming mouldy.

bamboo shoots *takenoko*
fibrous shoots, one of the most common ingredients in Asian cooking. Usually available in cans but sometimes fresh.

bonito flakes *katsuobushi*
dried bonito is shaved into flakes and is available in cellophane packs; larger, coarser flakes are used to make dashi while the finer shavings are used as a garnish. Keep flakes in an airtight container after opening.

breadcrumbs, japanese *panko*
available in two kinds: larger pieces and fine crumbs. Both have a lighter texture than Western-style breadcrumbs.

capsicum also known as bell pepper or, simply, pepper. Discard seeds and membranes before use.

chopsticks *hashi* Japanese chopsticks have more pointed ends than Chinese. They range from ornate, lacquered models to disposable pine or bamboo versions. Longer chopsticks are for cooking and are usually joined at the top with string so they can be hung up, or used for serving.

cooling tub *hangiri* or *handai*
the Japanese wooden tub in which cooked sushi rice is spread, cut, turned and cooled; must be washed and dried well after use to avoid becoming mouldy and discoloured.

cornflour also known as cornstarch, used as a thickening agent and for coating food.

daikon giant white radish, available fresh from Asian and western greengrocers.
PICKLED *takuan* or *oshinko* daikon pickled in rice bran and salt, is yellow, crunchy and very pungent. Used in sushi rolls and served as part of a plate of pickles to cleanse the palate between bites of food.

dashi traditionally, three types of dashi are used in Japanese cooking: katsuo-dashi, stock from dried bonito flakes; konbu-dashi, stock from dried kelp seaweed used for shabu-shabu (one-pot dish); and niboshi-dashi, stock from dried small sardines or anchovies. Dashi is used in clear soups, miso soups and various casserole dishes. Instant dashi is available in powder, granules and liquid concentrate.

eggplant vegetable also known as aubergine.

eggs some recipes in this book call for raw or barely cooked eggs; exercise caution if there is a salmonella problem in your area.

ginger *shoga* fresh ginger root.
PICKLED PINK *gari* sweet pink pickled ginger eaten with sushi and sashimi.
PICKLED RED *beni-shoga* savoury red pickled ginger is sometimes used as a filling in sushi rolls.

ginger grater grates more finely than Western graters to produce fresh ginger pulp, from which ginger juice can be extracted. Use a pastry brush to remove ginger.

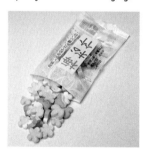

gluten, decorative *fu* small decorative shapes made from wheat gluten. Sold dried in packets, they are added directly to soups and one-pot dishes.

gourd *kampyo* gourd or calabash pith; sold dry, in packets, or cooked and seasoned, in cans or refrigerated packets. Softened, it's used as a filling in rolled sushi or as a decorative tie around food.

gyoza wrappers thin pastry circles made from wheat flour and used to enclose fillings for dumplings or pot stickers (gyoza). If unavailable, substitute gow gee wrappers.

knives Japanese knives are made either of carbon steel, which lends them a sharper edge but makes them more prone to rust, or stainless steel. A sashimi knife has a long, flexible blade.

lotus root *renkon*
actually a rhizome (like ginger), lotus is used in dishes such as tempura and salads. Scrape or peel to remove skin before use. Sold in cans, fresh and frozen.

mandoline a hand-operated implement with adjustable blades for thick to very thin slicing, shredding and cutting into straw-sized sticks. Ideal for shredding carrot and daikon, similar results will be achieved with the shredding mechanism of the food processor or a plastic V-slicer. As a last resort, use the coarse side of a grater.

mint, japanese *shiso*
also known as perilla or beefsteak plant; a member of the mint family. Red shiso is less aromatic and used mainly to colour and spice pickles.

miso fermented soybean paste. There are many types of miso, each with its own aroma, flavour, colour and texture; can be kept, airtight, up to a year in the refrigerator. Generally, the darker the miso, the saltier the taste and denser the texture. Salt-reduced miso is available.

BROWN OR DARK BROWN *karakuchi* also known as *aka miso*, saltiest miso, often more bitter in taste; has very thick texture.

LIGHT BROWN *amakuchi* also known as *chukara*. Mild or medium salty.

WHITE *shiro* sweet miso for salad dressings, sauces, soups.

YELLOW *shinshu* deep yellow, smooth miso; fairly salty but tart. Good for general cooking.

miso soup the base is a blend of dashi and miso paste with two or three added solid ingredients such as tofu and shiitake mushrooms. Ready-to-serve Instant Miso Soup is available from Japanese food stores and is sold like instant soup (just add boiling water). Four types are available: aka miso (brown), shiro miso (white), with wakame or tofu.

mustard, japanese *karashi* hot mustard available in ready-to-use paste in tubes or powder from Asian grocery stores.

omelette pan a square pan used for cooking tamago-yaki, an omelette which is used both as a sushi topping and in sushi rolls.

noodles
CELLOPHANE *harusame* dried saifun noodles, available from Asian grocery stores. Fine translucent bean thread noodles made from various starches, most commonly Chinese mung beans, potato and corn starch. Closest fresh substitute is shirataki.

GELATINOUS *shirataki* translucent jelly-like noodles made from starch of konnyaku, a yam-like root vegetable sometimes known as devil's tongue. Available in refrigerated packets. Closest dry substitute is harusame or rice vermicelli.

SOBA noodles made from various proportions of buckwheat flour, usually available dried but can be purchased fresh from local noodle makers.

SOMEN very fine, delicate, dried white noodles made from wheat.

UDON thick, wide wheat noodles, available both dried and fresh from most supermarkets and also at Asian food stores.

large one-pot

sushi fan

large sushi rice cooling tub

large bamboo mat

amboo inger rater

chopping board

square omelette pan

small bamboo mat

one-pot dishes flameproof earthenware or metal dishes for preparing sukiyaki, shabu-shabu and tempura. As a substitute, use a wok or flameproof casserole dish.

pepper, japanese *sansho* ground spice from the pod of the prickly ash; closely related to sichuan pepper.

SEVEN-SPICE MIX *shichimi togarashi*, based on hot peppers, sansho pepper, mandarin peel, black hemp or white poppy seeds, dried seaweed (nori) and white sesame seeds. Used to season casseroles, soups and noodles.

plain flour also known as all-purpose flour, contains no raising agent.

rice *kome* short- or medium-grain rice is most suitable for Japanese dishes.

KOSHIHIKARI rice, grown in Australia from Japanese seed, is perfect for sushi and is available in supermarkets.

NISHIKI rice is equally good for sushi. Grown in California, it's found here in Asian food stores.

rice paddle *shamoji* used to spread, cut through and turn sushi rice; wet it first to avoid the rice sticking to it.

rice vinegar *komezu* brewed from rice and milder than most western vinegars; very light and sweet. Used for sushi and salad dressings; can be substituted with cider vinegar, diluted with a little water.

SUSHI VINEGAR *su* special blend of rice vinegar, sugar and salt used to make sushi rice. Ready-to-use sushi vinegar is available in liquid or powdered form.

rice wine
MIRIN sweet rice wine for cooking; from a mixture of medium-grain rice, glutinous rice and distilled rice spirit which is matured for two months to result in its particular sweetness of flavour.

SAKE dry rice wine, a basic ingredient in many Japanese dishes. Special and first grade is for drinking while ryoriyo sake is made for cooking and has a lower alcohol content than drinking sake.

sauce
SUKIYAKI cooking sauce for sukiyaki (one-pot dish). Made from soy sauce, sugar, sake (dry rice wine) and mirin (sweet rice wine). Available in bottles from Asian grocery stores.

TEMPURA *hon tsuyu* dipping sauce to accompany tempura or use as a soup stock for noodles. Sold concentrated; dilute with water before use. Blend of soy sauce, mirin and dashi.

TERIYAKI traditional blend of soy sauce and mirin to brush over meat, poultry and seafood while grilling, or to glaze fish. Two types, thick and thin, are available from supermarkets as well as Asian grocery stores.

TONKATSU thick, fruity, spicy sauce served with deep-fried, crumbed pork (tonkatsu); also good with grilled or barbecued dishes. Similar to any commercial barbecue sauce.

WORCESTERSHIRE SAUCE, JAPANESE *wustaa* there are two types available, one similar to normal worcestershire and the other somewhat blander; both are made from varying proportions of vinegar, tomatoes, onions, carrots, garlic and spices.

seafood note that the seafood in sashimi and some sushi has not been cooked.

CRAB *kani* sometimes served raw as sashimi.

FISH, FLAKED *denbu* or *oboro* flaked cooked cod that has been coloured pink and sweetened, available in refrigerated packets; used in sushi rolls. Keep packet refrigerated and in an airtight container after opening.

FLYING FISH ROE *tobiuo ko* fine-grained, orange eggs of the flying fish; used as sushi filling and a topping for battleship sushi (gunkan-maki).

SALMON *sake* popular sashimi and sushi fish, having bright coral-orange colour, soft velvety texture and sweet rich flavour.

SALMON ROE *ikura* from ikra, the Russian word for caviar, perhaps why it is often mistakenly used as red caviar in cooking; most commonly used topping for battleship sushi (gunkan-maki).

SEAFOOD STICKS, JAPANESE a popular ingredient in sushi, in fact, one of the main ingredients in the ever-popular california rolls; buy the frozen Japanese product – it is of better quality and shreds more readily than Western-style seafood sticks.

SEA URCHIN *uni* a delicacy; has rich, nut-like taste. Its soft, oily texture is wrapped, together with a bite-sized rice ball, in seaweed (yaki-nori) to make battleship sushi (gunkan-maki).

TUNA *maguro* possibly the most popular fish used in Western sushi, because of its familiarity and its clean, non-fishy taste and velvety texture. Yellowfin and bluefin tuna are the varieties most used in sushi-making. The colour of tuna flesh varies from light pink to red, depending on what part of the fish the flesh comes from.

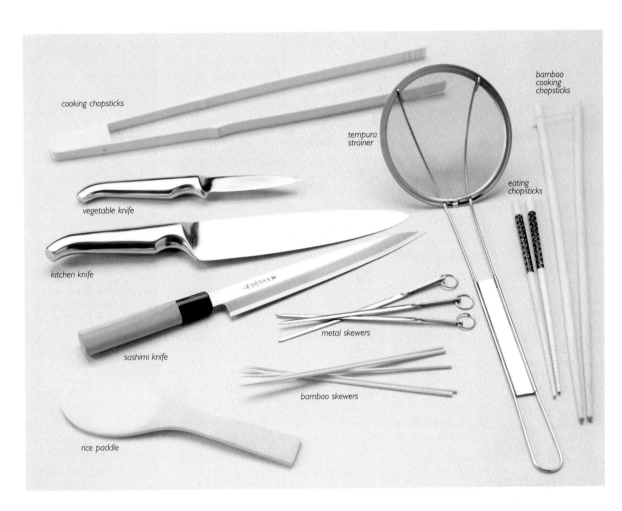

cooking chopsticks

bamboo cooking chopsticks

tempura strainer

eating chopsticks

vegetable knife

kitchen knife

sashimi knife

metal skewers

bamboo skewers

rice paddle

Back (left to right), fresh and dried seaweed (wakame); centre, kelp (konbu); right, shredded seaweed (ao-nori)

Back and centre, toasted seaweed sheets (yaki-nori); front, shredded seaweed (ao-nori)

seaweed

KELP *konbu* basis of dashi and simple boiled dishes to add slight flavour. Konbu should be thick and a glossy black or greenish brown in colour, and sometimes has a white powdery surface. Do not rinse but just wipe with a cloth or absorbent paper before use so as not to remove surface flavour; always remove konbu just before water boils because it can develop a bitter flavour if boiled. Cut the konbu pieces at intervals along edges to release extra flavour during the cooking process.

LAVER, DRIED *nori* dried laver or soft seaweed; can be toasted quickly on one side over high heat or under griller until it becomes slightly crisp.

TOASTED *yaki-nori* seaweed that is available already toasted in 10-sheet packages. Used in rolled sushi or crumbled over steamed rice with soy sauce. Can be refrigerated, frozen or stored in an airtight container and kept cool, dark and dry.

SHREDDED *ao-nori* small pieces of shredded dried laver seaweed used as an edible garnish.

DRIED *wakame* a bright-green lobe-leafed seaweed usually sold in dry form and used in soups and salads. It shouldn't be simmered for more than a minute as it loses nutrients and colour. Dried wakame must be softened by soaking in water for about 10 minutes; discard hard stems.

sesame seeds *goma* are the small oval seeds harvested from the tropical plant, sesamum indicum, which grows widely in India and other parts of Asia. Available raw (arai-goma), roasted (iri-goma), ground (suri-goma) or paste (neri-goma). The Middle Eastern condiment, tahini, can be substituted for grinding your own seeds to a paste.

WHITE *(shiro goma)*
BLACK *(kuro goma)*

shiitake mushrooms also sold as donko mushrooms; available fresh and dried. Have a unique meaty flavour, which is stronger when dried. To reconstitute dried, soak in warm water for 15 to 20 minutes; discard hard stems before use as they never soften. The soaking liquid can be added to soups and one-pots.
snow pea vegetable also known as mange tout (eat all).

soy sauce *shoyu*
a basic ingredient in many Japanese dishes. Kikkoman, a well-known and popular brand, is naturally brewed whereas many others are chemically made with additives. Keep refrigerated after opening. Different soy sauces have different strengths and tastes; for instance, Chinese soy is stronger and saltier than Japanese soy. Always use Japanese soy with Japanese food as the others are too strong and overpower the cuisines' intrinsic delicacy.
PONZU SHOYU soy sauce and ponzu citrus juice, blended, sometimes with mirin and sake (rice wines), available from Asian grocery stores.
JAPANESE *koikuchi shoyu* traditional Japanese soy sauce; lighter, less dense and less salty than Chinese soy sauce. Made with soy beans (cooked), wheat

(roasted and crushed) and brine, it is brewed then pressed and bottled. Better quality soy sauces require a six-month natural brewing process, and have no added artificial colourings, flavourings, preservatives or monosodium glutamate. Some soy sauces are wheat gluten-free and are suitable for consumption by people with coeliac disease.

LIGHT *usukuchi shoyu* lightly coloured soy sauce that's slightly saltier than koikuchi shoyu. Used in dishes in which the natural or original colour of the ingredients is to be maintained. It shouldn't be confused with salt-reduced soy sauce.
TAMARI predecessor of shoyu (soy sauce). Although traditional shoyu is made with nearly equal amounts of soy beans and wheat, tamari is normally made with soy beans and such a small amount of wheat that it is considered free from wheat gluten and thus suitable for coeliacs. Deep rich colour and unique flavour.
strainer, tempura *ami-shakushi* a very fine wire mesh scoop used to skim hot oil or broth while cooking dishes such as tempura. This utensil is also handy for straining used oil before storing.
sushi fan *uchiwa* flat fan made of paper or silk and stretched over bamboo ribs; used to cool sushi rice.
sushi mould *oshiwaku* wooden box used as a large mould for pressed sushi.

tofu also known as bean curd, an off-white, custard-like product made from the "milk" of crushed soy beans; comes fresh, as soft or firm, and processed, as fried or pressed sheets. Fresh tofu should be pressed under a weight such as a house brick for 25 minutes to remove excess moisture.

DEEP-FRIED BEAN CURD *abura-age* thin, deep-fried bean curd that can be opened to form a pouch; also available as seasoned bean curd pouches in packets or cans. *Atsu-age* is a thicker version of deep-fried bean curd.

wasabi Japanese horseradish.
POWDER comes in a can; mix with water to form a stiff paste. Once opened, keep dry and airtight.
PASTE comes in a tube ready to use. Refrigerate after opening.
zucchini variety of squash also known as courgette.

sashimi and sushi garnishes

Most Japanese dishes are garnished to give a contrast of both flavour and colour. They also give a sense of the seasons to dishes.

1 red maple radish

To make red maple radish, or momiji oroshi, dried chillies are grated with daikon for added flavour and colour. The finished product is said to resemble autumn maple leaves.

Using a chopstick, poke four holes in end of daikon. Seed chillies and push into each hole with chopstick. Grate the daikon and chillies in a circular motion with a Japanese or fine-toothed grater. Squeeze out excess liquid.

Shape into small mounds and place on side of serving dish or in the centre of dipping sauce.

2 wasabi leaf

Add enough water to wasabi powder to make a soft, spreadable paste; roll about 1 teaspoon of wasabi paste into a small ball then flatten and shape with fingers into leaf shape.

Lightly mark a central vein down the middle with a knife or toothpick, then side veins at a 45-degree angle. Place next to ginger rose on platters of sashimi and sushi.

3 pink pickled ginger rose

Lay pieces of gari (pink slices of pickled ginger) across chopping board, each one slightly overlapping the last.

Pick up edge nearest you; roll other end. Stand roll on its end; open slightly at top to resemble rose. Serve with a wasabi leaf as garnish.

sushi rice

sumeshi

The success of sushi largely depends on perfectly cooked sumeshi – cooled vinegared rice. Use short-grain rice such as Australian-grown koshihikari or the nishiki variety from California. These varieties have the ideal texture and consistency to just stick together without being gluggy. If you use medium-grain rice, you may need to add a little more water.

PREPARATION TIME 10 MINUTES (plus draining time)
COOKING TIME 12 MINUTES (plus standing time)

3 cups (600g) short-grain white rice
3 cups (750ml) water

SUSHI VINEGAR
1/2 cup (125ml) rice vinegar
1/4 cup (55g) sugar
1/2 teaspoon salt

1 Place rice in large bowl, fill with cold water, stir with hand. Drain; repeat process two or three times until water is almost clear. Drain rice in strainer or colander at least 30 minutes.

2 Meanwhile, prepare sushi vinegar.

3 **To cook rice in rice cooker:** place drained rice and the water in rice cooker, cover; switch onto "cook". When cooker automatically switches to "keep warm" position, allow rice to stand, covered, 10 minutes. **To cook rice in saucepan:** place drained rice and the water in medium saucepan, cover tightly; bring to a boil. Reduce heat; simmer, covered tightly, on low heat about 12 minutes or until water is absorbed. Remove from heat; allow rice to stand, covered, 10 minutes.

4 Spread rice in a large, non-metallic flat-bottomed bowl or tub (preferably wood). Using a rice paddle, a large flat wooden spoon or a plastic spatula, repeatedly slice through the rice at a sharp angle to break up lumps and separate grains, gradually pouring in the sushi vinegar at the same time. Not all of the vinegar may be required; the rice shouldn't become too wet or mushy.

5 Continue to slice (don't stir because it crushes the rice grains) with one hand, lifting and turning the rice from the outside into the centre (this action is similar to folding beaten egg whites into a cake or soufflé mixture).

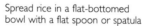

1 Spread rice in a flat-bottomed bowl with a flat spoon or spatula

2 Slice through rice to break up lumps and pour in vinegar

6 Meanwhile, using the other hand, fan the rice until it is almost cool; this will take about 5 minutes (an electric fan, on the low setting, can be used instead of a hand-held fan if you prefer). Do not over-cool rice or it will harden. Performing these two actions together will give you glossy, slightly sticky but still separate sushi rice. Keep the rice covered with a damp cloth to stop it drying out while making sushi.

sushi vinegar Stir combined vinegar, sugar and salt in small bowl until sugar dissolves. To make this mixture slightly less stringent, heat it gently just before using.

MAKES 9 CUPS

tip You can add either a little mirin or sake to the sushi vinegar mixture if you like, or you can use 1/2 cup (125ml) ready-made bottled sushi vinegar. Sushi vinegar can be made ahead and refrigerated in an airtight container.

3 Fan the rice to cool, either by hand or with an electric fan

sushi

Front row: handmade sushi (nigiri-zushi) made with salmon and tuna
Second row: large spiral rolls (futo-maki-zushi) and sushi inside-out rolls (yakiwa-maki-zushi) are both forms of maki-zushi
Third row: battleship and prawn handmade sushi (nigiri-zushi)
Back row: tuna rolls (tekka-maki-zushi)

Although sushi often includes raw fish, many other ingredients are also used with the cooled sushi rice, such as cooked seafood, fresh seasoned and/or pickled vegetables, seasoned omelette and tofu. Sushi comes in many forms and can be eaten with chopsticks or with your fingers.

The most common styles of sushi are:

1. sushi rolls (maki-zushi)

Maki is wrapped sushi with rice, fish and/or other ingredients enclosed in seaweed sheets (nori) then rolled into shape using a special bamboo mat. Maki-zushi is served with soy sauce, pink pickled ginger (gari) and wasabi. There are several different varieties of maki-zushi:

small sushi (hoso-maki-zushi)

This is a slender roll with one or two fillings. It is served cut into six small pieces. Popular **kappa-maki-zushi** has a simple cucumber filling and **tekka-maki-zushi** has a tuna filling.

large spiral rolls (futo-maki-zushi)

Made from a whole sheet of toasted seaweed (yaki-nori), this thick sushi usually contains several different ingredients in the filling. A variation of futo-maki-zushi is the "inside-out" roll, **ura-maki-zushi**, where the rice is outside the filling.

sushi hand-rolls (temaki-zushi)

This filled hand-roll looks like an ice-cream cone and is eaten as soon as it's made, as it doesn't keep well.

2. handmade sushi (nigiri-zushi)

Nigiri-zushi is perhaps the most familiar type of sushi to us, and is the most common kind eaten in sushi bars all over the world. Wasabi-swiped sushi rice is moulded into a small oval then a slice of cooked or raw seafood, vegetable or omelette is hand-pressed on top. Fish roe or sea urchin are sometimes made into a nigiri-type sushi called **gunkan-maki-zushi**, or "battleship" sushi due to its imposing shape. Oval or round bite-sized rice balls are wrapped in a strip of toasted seaweed which rises just above the rice to enclose the filling. Dip in soy before eating.

3. scattered sushi (chirashi-zushi)

This is another good sushi for beginners since the fish and vegetables are simply laid (scattered) on top of the sushi rice and no rolling or moulding is required.

4. pressed zushi (oshi-zushi)

This sushi is made by pressing rice into a large wooden box (oshiwaku), topping it with cooked, cured or salted seafood, then cutting it into portions. It can be made ahead.

5. seasoned tofu pouches (inari-zushi)

Legend has it that inari is named after the fox who guards the grain harvest. One of the best-known kinds of sushi, inari is good for beginners because the rice is enclosed in a deep-fried seasoned bean curd pouch (sweetened abura-age) that holds together well. It is seldom made with raw fish so it is a good choice for timid palates. The seasoned pouches (sweetened abura-age) are available at Asian food stores in cans and packets. Unseasoned abura-age pouches are sold frozen.

6. california rolls

A popular recent invention from America, the name is a reference to the filling, rather than the shape of the sushi. These rolls usually contain cooked crab meat, prawn or seafood stick, avocado, mayonnaise, cucumber and sometimes flying fish roe.

tips and traditions

■ It is quite acceptable to eat sushi with the fingers as well as chopsticks.

■ Usually, only one or two fillings are used in small rolls and up to five or six in large ones. To use more fillings, cut the ingredients more finely.

■ Sushi is always served with pink pickled ginger slices (gari) and japanese soy sauce. Although sushi has wasabi in it already, serve extra for personal tastes. Traditionally, wasabi is not served with pickled or seasoned fillings.

■ Keep remaining pieces of seaweed covered and dry while making sushi because they'll soften and wrinkle when exposed to the moisture in the air.

■ To help keep filling in the centre of the roll, build up a mound of rice in front of the uncovered strip of the toasted seaweed.

Building up rice in front of the uncovered strip of seaweed

■ If rolls are overly full, they could split or not stay rolled tightly. Thicker rolls can be made by turning a rectangular seaweed piece so that the short side runs parallel to the grain of the bamboo mat. This allows more filling to be used but the result is a shorter roll.

■ Ideally, sushi should be assembled as close to serving time as possible, as the seaweed absorbs moisture from the air and rice and could split.

Rolls can be made and kept for up to 2 hours if covered in plastic wrap. Cut into pieces just before serving to prevent the rice from drying out.

■ If rolls are over-filled and splitting, place another half sheet of seaweed (for thin rolls) or full sheet (for large rolls) on the bamboo mat, shiny-side down. Sit uncut roll with split face-down on seaweed; lightly dampen both long sides of seaweed then, using mat, roll away from you, as for a sushi roll. Cut into six or eight pieces, starting from centre.

Patching up a split, over-filled roll

■ Use a split thin roll as the filling for a thick roll, using a full sheet of nori.

■ Although a sheet of plastic wrap, foil or baking paper can be used to make sushi rolls, a bamboo mat makes the job much easier.

■ If making sushi for a group that includes children, it's wise to make some vegetarian and some without wasabi. Simply serve small bowls of wasabi alongside the platters of sushi – with a warning to your guests that it is not guacamole!

■ Never serve large bowls of soy sauce for dipping; not only is this considered bad manners but, since pieces of rice always fall into the dish, you end up with a mess and waste all that remaining soy.

■ Dipping sauces should complement the fish they accompany. As a rule, the more delicate the fish, the lighter the seasoning of the dipping sauce. Ponzu sauce (lemon and soy) suits a subtle flavoured, non-oily, thinly sliced fish, but thicker cuts of firm white fish require a stronger soy flavour. Miso paste mixed with a little vinegar helps disguise the muddy flavour of some fish, and the vinegar also slightly tenderises the fish.

■ Remember: there are never any mistakes when making sushi – just new designs! If the filling falls forward as the mat is rolled and ends up at the far edge of the rice, simply shape each piece of sushi gently with fingers into a teardrop shape with the filling at the narrow end. Arrange these pieces in a circle, fillings to the centre, and add a garnish in the middle – a sushi flower!

Shaping sushi into "teardrops" to make petals of a sushi flower

■ And if it really seems too hard, have a sushi party. Prepare rice, seaweed and a wide assortment of filling ingredients, then get everybody to make their own hand-rolls (temaki) – no skill and no recipe required, and someone may come up with an absolutely delicious unusual combination of filling ingredients!

did you know?

The essential difference, as far as non-Japanese cooks are concerned, between sushi and sashimi is that the fish in sashimi (which simply translates as "raw") is not accompanied with rice, although it is, like sushi, dipped in soy sauce and eaten with wasabi and ginger. Sashimi and sushi fish are carefully selected, handled, kept and prepared by specially trained chefs to guarantee that only the very freshest product makes it to the table. At market, the fish should always be labelled "sashimi quality".

tuna rolls
tekka-maki-zushi

PREPARATION TIME 20 MINUTES

Cutting one folded sheet of seaweed in half lengthways

Gently "raking" rice evenly over seaweed

Picking up mat using thumbs and index fingers

Cutting across aligned halves of roll with a very sharp knife

Tekka translates loosely as gambling den, for which this sushi roll was first devised, because wrapping the rice in nori prevented the players' fingers sticking to the cards. One of the best known of all sushi types, tekka-maki-zushi is also one of the simplest to prepare and thus the perfect example to use for showing how to make rolled sushi.

3 sheets toasted seaweed (yaki-nori)
medium bowl filled with cold water,
   with 1 tablespoon rice vinegar added
3 cups prepared sushi rice (see page 12)
1 tablespoon wasabi
200g piece sashimi tuna, cut into
   1cm-thick strips
2 tablespoons pink pickled ginger (gari)
1/4 cup (60ml) japanese soy sauce

1 Fold one sheet of seaweed in half lengthways, parallel with lines marked on rough side of seaweed; cut along fold. Place a half sheet, shiny-side down, lengthways across bamboo mat about 2cm from edge of mat closest to you.

2 Dip fingers in bowl of vinegared water; shake off excess. Pick up about 1/2 cup of the rice, squeeze into oblong shape, place across centre of seaweed.

3 Wet fingers again, then, working from left to right, gently "rake" rice evenly over seaweed, leaving 2cm strip on far end of seaweed uncovered. Build up rice in front of uncovered seaweed strip to form mound to keep filling in place (see page 15).

4 Using finger, swipe a dab of wasabi across centre of rice, flattening it out evenly.

5 Place tuna strips, end to end, in a row over wasabi across centre of rice.

6 Starting with edge closest to you, pick up mat, using thumb and index fingers of both hands; use remaining fingers to hold filling in place as you begin to roll mat away from you. Roll forward, pressing gently but tightly, wrapping seaweed around rice and fillings.

7 When roll is completed, a strip of uncovered seaweed will stick to the bottom of the roll to form join; exert gentle pressure to make the roll slightly square in shape.

8 Unroll mat; place sushi roll, join-down, on board. Wipe very sharp knife with damp cloth then cut roll in half. Turn one half piece around 180 degrees so that the two cut ends of each half are aligned. Slice through both rolls together twice, to give a total of six bite-sized pieces, wiping knife between each cut.

9 Working quickly, repeat process with remaining seaweed halves, rice and tuna, using a dab of wasabi with each. Serve tuna rolls with remaining wasabi, pickled ginger and sauce served separately.

MAKES 6 ROLLS (36 PIECES)

suggestions for alternative fillings
- thin strips of avocado and salmon
- cucumber and pickled plum
- crab stick and avocado
- cucumber (kappa-maki)

large spiral rolls
futo-maki-zushi

PREPARATION TIME 20 MINUTES

Placing rice across centre of seaweed with vinegared fingers

Make sure that fillings extend to both ends of rice

Using mat to wrap seaweed gently around rice and fillings

Unrolling mat to place sushi roll, join-down, on board

Unlike their thinner maki-zushi relatives, futo-maki-zushi are thick sushi rolls usually containing between four and six ingredients in the filling. These fillings are just as often selected for their colour and texture as for their taste, to make both a complementary and a satisfying whole. The filling ingredients we've used here are often seen in many sushi restaurants' futo-maki-zushi, but you can use many others – see our selection below.

4 sheets toasted seaweed (yaki-nori)
medium bowl filled with cold water,
    with 1 tablespoon rice vinegar
4 cups prepared sushi rice (see page 12)
2 tablespoons wasabi
4 strips 5mm x 18cm pickled
    daikon (takuan)
200g piece sashimi tuna, cut into
    1cm-thick strips
1 lebanese cucumber (130g), halved,
    seeded, sliced thinly
1/2 portion thick omelette (see page 70),
    cut into 1cm-wide strips
4 strips seasoned gourd (seasoned kampyo)
1/4 cup (20g) dried flaked cod (denbu)
2 tablespoons pink pickled ginger (gari)
1/4 cup (60ml) japanese soy sauce

1 Place one sheet of seaweed, shiny-side down, lengthways across bamboo mat about 2cm from edge of mat closest to you .

2 Dip fingers of one hand in bowl of vinegared water; shake off excess; pick up about a quarter of the rice, place across centre of seaweed sheet.

3 Wet fingers again, then, working from left to right, gently "rake" rice evenly over seaweed, leaving 2cm strip on far side of seaweed uncovered. Build up rice in front of uncovered strip to form mound to keep filling in place.

4 Using a finger, swipe a dab of wasabi across centre of rice, flattening it out evenly. Place about a quarter of the pickled daikon, tuna, cucumber, omelette, gourd and dried cod in a row over wasabi across centre of rice; make sure that fillings extend to both ends of rice.

5 Starting with edge closest to you, pick up mat using thumb and index fingers of both hands; use remaining fingers to hold filling in place as you begin to roll mat away from you. Roll forward, pressing gently but tightly, wrapping seaweed around rice and fillings.

6 When roll is completed, join of seaweed should be on the bottom of the roll; exert gentle pressure to make the roll slightly square in shape.

7 Unroll mat; place sushi roll, join-down, on board. Wipe very sharp knife with damp cloth then cut roll in half. Turn one half piece around 180 degrees so that the two cut ends of each half are aligned. Slice both rolls together in half then these halves in half again, to give a total of eight bite-sized pieces, wiping knife between each cut.

8 Working quickly, repeat process with remaining seaweed, rice and filling ingredients, using a dab of wasabi with each. Serve spiral rolls with remaining wasabi, pickled ginger and sauce, served separately.

MAKES 4 ROLLS (32 PIECES)

suggestions for alternative fillings

■ snow pea sprouts, japanese seafood sticks, red pickled ginger, cucumber, thick omelette (see page 70)
■ cooked crab meat, mayonnaise, cucumber, avocado, fish roe, shredded lettuce
■ spring onion, shredded carrot, capsicum, avocado, snow pea sprouts
■ prawns, salmon roe, bamboo shoots, green onion, avocado

inside-out rolls

ura-maki-zushi

PREPARATION TIME 20 MINUTES

Sprinkling sushi rice with black sesame seeds

Lifting and turning mat so that seaweed faces upwards

Rolling mat and plastic wrap around rice and filling

Unrolling mat, leaving roll in plastic wrap

2 sheets toasted seaweed (yaki-nori), folded parallel with lines on rough side of seaweed, cut in half
medium bowl filled with cold water, with 1 tablespoon rice vinegar
4 cups prepared sushi rice (see page 12)
2 tablespoons flying fish roe
1 teaspoon toasted black sesame seeds
1¹/₂ tablespoons wasabi
¹/₂ lebanese cucumber (65g), halved, seeded, sliced thinly
4 large cooked prawns (200g), shelled, deveined, halved lengthways
4 strips 5mm x 18cm pickled daikon (takuan)
1¹/₂ tablespoons red pickled ginger (beni-shoga)
2 tablespoons pink pickled ginger (gari)
¹/₄ cup (60ml) japanese soy sauce

1 Place one half-sheet seaweed lengthways across bamboo mat about 2cm from edge of mat closest to you. Dip fingers of one hand in bowl of vinegared water, shake off excess; pick up a quarter of the rice, press onto seaweed then, working from left to right, gently "rake" rice to cover seaweed completely and evenly (see page 16).

2 Sprinkle a quarter of the roe and seeds over rice then cover rice completely with a piece of plastic wrap. Carefully lift mat; turn over so seaweed faces up; place back on bamboo mat about 2cm from the edge. Using finger, swipe a dab of wasabi across centre of seaweed, then top with about a quarter of the cucumber, prawn, pickled daikon and red pickled ginger, making certain that filling extends to both ends of seaweed.

3 Pick up the edge of the bamboo mat and plastic wrap with index finger and thumb; place remaining fingers on filling to hold in place as you roll mat tightly away from you, wrapping rice around filling. Press roll gently and continue rolling forward to complete the roll. Unroll mat and keep roll in plastic wrap.

4 Wipe sharp knife with damp cloth; cut roll, still in plastic wrap, in half, then each half into quarters, to make eight pieces, wiping knife between each cut. Remove plastic wrap and serve inside-out rolls with remaining wasabi, pink pickled ginger and sauce.

MAKES 4 ROLLS (32 PIECES)

tips Make two small cuts in the underside of the prawns so they lie flat.

Place dried flaked cod (denbu) or finely chopped fresh herbs on outside of rolls.

Keep finished inside-out rolls wrapped in plastic wrap, uncut, until ready to serve to prevent them from drying out.

suggestions for alternative fillings

■ cucumber slices, sashimi salmon, avocado and sesame seeds

■ japanese crab sticks, red pickled ginger, snow pea sprouts and cucumber

■ tuna, avocado, cucumber and green onion (green part only)

■ prawn, cucumber, avocado and lettuce, with flying fish roe on outside

■ canned or fresh salmon, wasabi mayonnaise, green onion, asparagus

■ shredded carrot, avocado, green onion, snow pea sprouts

sushi hand-rolls

temaki-zushi

PREPARATION TIME 30 MINUTES

Dipping fingers in vinegared water with seaweed across palm

Using finger to swipe wasabi mayonnaise along groove in rice

Folding sides of seaweed over filling to form a cone

This is a great idea for a party – and very easy on the host! All the required slicing and chopping can be done before the guests arrive, and everyone will get a kick out of making their own sushi rolls, picking and choosing their favourite filling ingredients. Sushi hand-rolls don't keep very well, another reason for making and eating them at the same time. Below, we give you the ingredients you need to make the classic california roll, but there is virtually no end of filling possibilities (see suggestions at the end of recipe).

3 cups prepared sushi rice (see page 12)
4 sheets toasted seaweed (yaki-nori)
1 large avocado (320g)
1 tablespoon lemon juice
2 tablespoons mayonnaise
1 teaspoon wasabi
4 japanese seafood sticks,
  quartered lengthways
1 lebanese cucumber (130g), halved, seeded,
  cut lengthways into 16 strips
1 teaspoon toasted black sesame seeds
1/2 cup (125ml) japanese soy sauce
2 tablespoons pink pickled ginger (gari)

1   Place sushi rice in non-metallic serving bowl; cover with damp cloth. Cut each sheet of seaweed into quarters; cover with plastic wrap until ready to serve (seaweed must be kept covered because it softens and wrinkles if left exposed to the moisture in the air). Slice avocado thinly, brush with lemon juice to stop it discolouring; cover. Combine mayonnaise and wasabi in small bowl; cover.

2   For each roll: place a quarter sheet of the seaweed, shiny-side down, diagonally across palm of left hand, then dip fingers of right hand in bowl of vinegared water. Shaking off excess water, pick up about 2 tablespoons of the rice, placing it in the centre of seaweed. Using the fingers of your right hand, "rake" rice towards top corner of seaweed, making a slight groove down the middle of the rice for the filling.

3   Using one finger of right hand, swipe a dab of wasabi mayonnaise along the groove in rice, topping it with a slice each of avocado, seafood stick and cucumber, then a small sprinkle of seeds.

4   Fold one side of seaweed over to stick to rice; fold other side of seaweed over the first to form a cone. Tip of cone can be folded back to hold cone shape securely.

5   Dip hand-roll in sauce; top with a slice of pickled ginger, if desired, and eat immediately.

MAKES 16 HAND-ROLLS

tip Hand-rolls can be made with half sheets of seaweed, if preferred.

suggestions for alternative fillings

▪ cucumber, smoked salmon, avocado and fresh dill tips
▪ shelled cooked prawns, pickled daikon (takuan), snow pea sprouts and green onion
▪ sashimi tuna, salmon roe, avocado, shredded lettuce and cucumber
▪ sashimi salmon, wasabi mayonnaise, green onion and cooked asparagus
▪ shredded carrot, avocado, green onion, snow pea sprouts and thick omelette (see page 70)

other ingredients that can be combined in fillings

▪ grilled eggplant slices, seasoned deep-fried tofu strips, tomato, spinach leaves, capsicum strips, chives, snow pea strips, seasoned gourd (seasoned kampyo), dried flaked cod (denbu), bamboo shoots, green beans, flying fish roe

hand-moulded sushi

nigiri-zushi

Slicing tuna thinly

Nigiri-zushi is the sushi we're probably most familiar with. Here are a few things you should know before making these delicious morsels:

■ *Don't make the pieces too big; each should only make a single mouthful.*

■ *The slice of fish should serve as a roof over the rice; no matter how big or small the ball of rice is, it never protrudes beyond the fish.*

■ *Use slightly more wasabi for oily fish, such as tuna and salmon, and less for milder seafood such as white fish (trevally, kingfish, etc), prawns and squid.*

■ *Fish should always only be sliced just before making sushi.*

■ *If correctly formed, nigiri-zushi should be able to be eaten upside down using fingers, or on its side if eaten with chopsticks; it's the fish and not the rice which is to be dipped in soy sauce.*

Gently squeezing and shaping rice into rounded rectangle

Using fingers to push rice and fish together

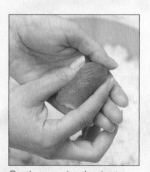

Gently squeezing the rice to straighten the sides

**medium bowl filled with cold water,
  with 1 tablespoon rice vinegar**
3 cups prepared sushi rice (see page 12)
350g sashimi tuna, sliced thinly
2 teaspoons wasabi
1/4 cup (60ml) japanese soy sauce

1 Dip fingers of both hands in bowl of vinegared water, shake off excess; pick up about 1 tablespoon of rice with your right hand, gently squeezing and shaping it into a rectangle shape with rounded edges.

2 Pick up one slice of fish with the index finger and thumb of the left hand. Using tip of right-hand index finger, scoop up a dab of wasabi; spread wasabi along centre of fish.

3 Bend fingers of left hand to form cup to hold fish; place rice shape on fish.

4 Move left thumb to top end of rice shape to stop rice being pushed off fish; use right-hand index and middle fingers to gently push rice shape and fish together.

5 Turn sushi piece over so fish is on top, gently push fish against rice with right-hand index and middle fingers; left thumb should remain at top end of rice to stop it being pushed out.

6 With thumb on one side of rice and index finger on the other, gently squeeze rice to straighten the sides.

7 Using right-hand index finger and thumb, turn sushi 180 degrees and push fish against rice again with right-hand index and middle fingers.

8 Serve hand-moulded sushi with sauce in a separate bowl.

MAKES 30

tip To keep fish on the rice, place a 1cm-wide strip of toasted seaweed (yaki-nori) around centre of sushi piece with ends tucked underneath; moisture from the rice will hold seaweed in place.

suggestions for alternative toppings

■ sashimi-quality fish, squid, cuttlefish, cooked prawns, thick omelette (see page 70), blanched snow peas, cooked asparagus, avocado

seasoned tofu pouches

inari-zushi

PREPARATION TIME 15 MINUTES
COOKING TIME 15 MINUTES

Gently pushing fingers into each corner of pouch to open it

Pushing rice loosely into pouch

Folding over sides of pouch to enclose filling

Ready-made seasoned bean-curd skins and seasoned gourd (seasoned kampyo) strips are available from Asian specialist grocery stores.

**8 seasoned fried bean curd pouches
(sweetened abura-age)**
1 teaspoon toasted black sesame seeds
**1 lebanese cucumber (130g), halved,
seeded, diced finely**
1$\frac{1}{2}$ cups prepared sushi rice (see page 12)
**medium bowl filled with cold water,
with 1 tablespoon rice vinegar**
8 strips seasoned gourd (seasoned kampyo)
1 teaspoon red pickled ginger (beni-shoga)

1 Carefully cut open pouches on one side, gently pushing fingers into each corner to form pouch.

2 Reserve a few of the seeds for garnish; fold remaining seeds and cucumber through rice.

3 Dip fingers of right hand in bowl of vinegared water, shake off excess. Pick up about an eighth of the rice with right hand; gently and loosely fit it into one pouch, being careful not to overfill or tear pouch and to push rice into pouch's corners.

4 Fold one side of pouch down over rice; fold the other side over the first and turn the pouch over so the join is underneath.

5 Tie a strip of gourd around pouch with a loose knot on top; garnish with a little red pickled ginger and reserved sesame seeds. Repeat with remaining ingredients.

MAKES 8

sashimi

Sashimi is usually eaten at the beginning of a meal, presumably before the tastebuds have been dulled by other flavours.

Outside of Japan, the fish to use for sashimi and sushi should be those that are in season and labelled "sashimi quality", as a guarantee of correct health and handling standards. This fish should have a firm texture, a pleasant sea-smell (but not "fishy"), bright red gills and, ideally, bright, clear eyes, although the eyes of a perfectly fresh fish can turn cloudy due to contact with ice.

Either buy whole fish and fillet it yourself, or select fillets or blocks (of tuna) which can then be sliced for you by the fishmonger, if preferred. Fish slices discolour quickly once cut, so it is preferable to slice it as close to serving time as possible. Incidentally, meat from the same tuna can be three different shades of red or pink, depending on which part of the fish it is from.

If you choose to cut the fish yourself, always use a very sharp knife with a long, flexible, very thin blade. Never "saw" the fish; cut it in a single movement, pulling knife down and towards your body.

Dipping sauces and garnishes are not purely decorative, but enhance the flavour of fish. The giant white radish known as daikon aids digestion and cuts the oiliness of the fish, while pickled ginger cleanses the palate between bites of different fish. It is best to place a tiny amount of wasabi, the hot green Japanese horseradish, directly on each piece of fish and then dip it into the sauce. Mixing wasabi into the dipping sauce only diminishes both flavours.

When serving mixed sashimi, it is important that the different types of fish do not touch one another; arrange slightly apart on the plates or separate with fresh or artificial leaves, such as japanese mint (shiso), bamboo, camellia, flat-leaf parsley or lemon leaves. Thin, twisted slices of lemon are especially suitable to separate oily fish.

In Japan, many things (from a teacup set to a serving of sashimi) are traditionally presented or served in odd-numbered (rather than even) quantities. However, there are no absolutes about serving size; it depends on the number and size of the other dishes being served during the meal.

tuna sashimi

PREPARATION TIME 10 MINUTES
(plus soaking time)

The most important step in successful sashimi making is the guarantee that you start with absolutely the freshest of fish; here, we serve sufficient sashimi-quality tuna to serve four as an entree. Use a mandoline (if you own one) to shred the daikon. You'll need a piece of daikon about 7cm long and 5cm in diameter for this recipe.

³/4 cup (200g) finely shredded daikon
400g sashimi tuna (maguro)
2 teaspoons wasabi
2 tablespoons pink pickled ginger (gari)
¹/3 cup (80ml) japanese soy sauce

1 Soak daikon in bowl of iced water for 15 minutes; drain well.

2 Place tuna on chopping board; using very sharp knife, cut 6mm slices at right angles to the grain of the fish, holding the piece of skinned fish with your fingers and slicing with the knife almost vertical to the board.

3 Divide tuna slices among serving plates; mound equal amounts of daikon next to tuna.

4 Garnish plates with equal amounts of mounded wasabi and pickled ginger; serve with separate bowl of soy sauce.

SERVES 4

Shredding the peeled daikon as finely as possible

Cutting 6mm slices straight down as knife is pulled forward

sashimi rolls

PREPARATION TIME 20 MINUTES

Sharpening knife using a steel

We used a combination of red (salmon), oily (tuna) and white (snapper) fish for this recipe, but you could also use trevally or various other types so long as all are labelled sashimi-quality at your fishmonger or market. Ask your fishmonger to slice it thinly for you if you prefer not to do so yourself.

200g sashimi fish
1/2 lebanese cucumber (65g), halved lengthways
1/4 medium red capsicum (50g)
1 green onion (green part only)
1/4 cup (60ml) japanese soy sauce

Trimming vegetables to appropriate size

1 Sharpen knife using a steel; wipe knife. Cut fish into paper-thin slices.

2 Remove and discard seeds from cucumber. Remove and discard seeds and membrane from capsicum. Cut cucumber, capsicum and onion into long thin strips; trim strips to approximately the same size as the width of the fish slices.

3 Place one fish slice on board; place one or two pieces of each vegetable at one end. Roll fish to enclose filling; repeat with remaining fish and filling. Serve sashimi rolls with soy sauce in a separate bowl.

MAKES 18 ROLLS

Rolling up fish slices

tip A toasted seaweed sheet (yaki-nori), or a few garlic chives or blanched spinach leaves, can also be used, trimmed to the same size as each piece of fish. Rolls can be "tied" with chives, if desired.

Cutting through salmon with knife at 45-degree angle

Making centre of salmon rose

Encircling centre of rose with additional "petals" of fish

sashimi salmon with lemon

PREPARATION TIME 20 MINUTES (plus standing time)
COOKING TIME 5 MINUTES

Gari, finely sliced pale-pink pickled ginger, is used both as a garnish and a palate freshener when eating sushi and sashimi. Use young small leaves from a rose bush as an (inedible) garnish or, if you prefer, substitute shiso (japanese mint) leaves, arranging them to look like flowers. You'll need a piece of daikon about 15cm long and 5cm in diameter for this recipe.

1¹/₂ cups (360g) finely shredded daikon
1 small carrot (70g), finely shredded
400g sashimi salmon
2 teaspoons wasabi
1 tablespoon pink pickled ginger (gari)

LEMON DIPPING SAUCE
¹/₂ cup (125ml) rice vinegar
¹/₄ cup (55g) caster sugar
1 teaspoon light soy sauce
¹/₄ teaspoon finely grated lemon rind
1 green onion (green part only), chopped finely

1 Place daikon and carrot in separate bowls of iced water; stand 15 minutes. Drain daikon and carrot; combine and arrange in mounds on serving plates.

2 Meanwhile, place knife at 45-degree angle to edge of salmon fillet; slice finely. Cover salmon slices with plastic wrap to prevent drying out. Roll one slice of salmon tightly then wrap three or four salmon slices around upright rolled piece until it resembles a rose. Repeat with remaining salmon. You will have approximately 12 roses.

3 Divide salmon roses among serving plates, standing upright, next to daikon and carrot on plate.

4 Make wasabi leaves (see page 11), arrange on serving plates; serve with pickled ginger and lemon dipping sauce in separate bowls.

lemon dipping sauce Heat vinegar, sugar and sauce in small saucepan, stirring, until sugar dissolves. Remove from heat, add rind; stand 10 minutes. Strain sauce into serving dish; discard rind. Sprinkle sauce with onion.

SERVES 4

sashimi tuna and wasabi salad

Cubing tuna

PREPARATION TIME 15 MINUTES

Beni-shoga is a dark-red pickled ginger which has been cured first in salt, then pickled in vinegar. Toast sesame seeds in a heated small frying pan without oil, stirring pan constantly. When seeds begin to pop, remove from heat.

400g sashimi tuna
1 medium avocado (250g)
1 cup (300g) mayonnaise
1 tablespoon wasabi
1 teaspoon lemon juice
6 green onions (green part only), sliced finely
4 iceberg lettuce leaves
1 teaspoon toasted black sesame seeds
1 tablespoon red pickled ginger (beni-shoga)

1 Cut tuna and peeled avocado into 1.5cm cubes; place in large bowl with combined mayonnaise, wasabi and juice. Add all but 2 tablespoons of the onion; toss tuna mixture gently to combine.

2 Divide tuna mixture among lettuce leaves in serving bowls; sprinkle with sesame seeds and remaining onion. Serve pickled ginger in separate bowl.

SERVES 4

tip Instead of topping the salad with sesame seeds and green onion, try using finely shredded toasted seaweed (yaki-nori).

Slicing the green onions thinly on the diagonal

marinated sashimi salmon

Cutting salmon into strips

PREPARATION TIME 20 MINUTES (plus marinating time)

Toast sesame seeds in a heated small frying pan without oil, stirring pan constantly. When seeds brown lightly and begin to pop, remove from heat.

500g sashimi salmon
2 teaspoons grated fresh ginger
1 clove garlic, crushed
1 teaspoon brown sugar
2 tablespoons japanese soy sauce
1/2 cup (125ml) sake
4 green onions (green part only), chopped finely
2 teaspoons toasted white sesame seeds

1 Slice salmon into 1cm strips.

2 Combine ginger, garlic, sugar, sauce, sake and half of the onion in medium bowl; stir until sugar dissolves. Add salmon; stir to coat in marinade. Cover bowl tightly; refrigerate 30 minutes.

3 Mound undrained salmon on serving platter; sprinkle with sesame seeds and remaining onion.

SERVES 4

Sprinkling sesame seeds and green onion over salmon

sashimi tuna salad with miso dressing

PREPARATION TIME 20 MINUTES (plus marinating time)
COOKING TIME 5 MINUTES

Tuna can be cut into cubes or finely sliced for this recipe

Patting the fish completely dry before tossing with the dressing

350g sashimi tuna
2 tablespoons sushi vinegar (see page 12)
4 green onions (green part only), chopped finely

MISO DRESSING
2 tablespoons white miso
1 tablespoon mirin
1 tablespoon sake
1 tablespoon sugar
2 tablespoons rice vinegar
1 teaspoon japanese soy sauce
$1/4$ teaspoon japanese mustard

1 Cut tuna into 2cm cubes or slice thinly. Place in medium bowl with vinegar; stand, covered, 15 minutes.

2 Drain tuna, discard marinade. Pat tuna dry with absorbent paper; place in medium bowl with chilled miso dressing. Toss gently to combine; divide among serving bowls, sprinkle with onion. Serve with wasabi or japanese mustard, if desired.

miso dressing Simmer miso, mirin, sake and sugar in small saucepan, stirring, until sugar dissolves. Remove from heat; stand 10 minutes then stir in vinegar, sauce and mustard. Refrigerate, covered, until required.

SERVES 4

tip Sashimi salmon may be used instead of tuna.

soups

miso soup with pork and green beans

PREPARATION TIME 15 MINUTES • COOKING TIME 10 MINUTES

Extracting juice from the grated fresh ginger

Adding pork to broth

Ginger juice can be obtained by squeezing grated fresh green (that is, young) ginger into a sieve set over a bowl. A piece of ginger measuring approximately 10cm in length will yield 2 tablespoons of grated ginger; this amount of grated ginger should in turn yield the 2 teaspoons of juice used in this recipe.

1 litre (4 cups) secondary dashi (see page 117)
100g pork fillet, sliced thinly
8 green beans, cut into 2cm lengths
1/4 cup (75g) red miso paste (karakuchi)
2 teaspoons fresh ginger juice
2 green onions, chopped finely

1 Bring dashi to a boil in medium saucepan. Add pork and beans; return to a boil. Reduce heat; simmer, uncovered, 2 minutes.

2 Place miso in small bowl; gradually add 1 cup (250ml) of the hot dashi, stirring, until miso dissolves. Add to saucepan, stir to combine. Bring just to a boil; remove immediately from heat.

3 Divide soup among serving bowls; stir 1/2 teaspoon ginger juice into each bowl, sprinkle with onion.

SERVES 4

tip Don't overcook soup after miso is added or some of the delicate flavour will be lost.

vegetable soup

PREPARATION TIME 10 MINUTES
COOKING TIME 15 MINUTES

*Daikon is a giant long white radish with a sweet fresh
taste and crisp texture. In Japan, it is often served as an
accompaniment, either pickled or raw. Shichimi togarashi,
literally seven-flavoured chilli, is a much-used spice mixture.*

3cm x 5cm piece daikon (60g)
1 small potato (120g)
1 small carrot (70g)
2 green onions
60g green beans
2 teaspoons vegetable oil
1 litre (4 cups) secondary dashi (see page 117)
1¹/₂ tablespoons japanese soy sauce
2 fresh shiitake mushrooms, quartered
¹/₂ x 227g can sliced bamboo shoots, rinsed, drained
1 teaspoon seven-spice mix (shichimi togarashi)

1   Quarter daikon and potato; slice thinly. Halve carrot
    lengthways; slice thinly. Slice onions diagonally into
    1cm pieces. Slice beans diagonally into 2cm pieces.

2   Heat oil in large saucepan; cook daikon, potato and
    carrot, stirring, until browned lightly.

3   Add dashi and sauce, bring to a boil. Reduce heat;
    simmer, uncovered, about 5 minutes or until carrot is
    just tender. Add onion, beans, mushrooms and bamboo
    shoots; simmer, uncovered, about 2 minutes or until
    vegetables are just tender.

4   Divide soup among serving bowls; sprinkle with
    seven-spice mix.

SERVES 4

tip   You can substitute chicken stock for dashi.

serving suggestion   You can add 100g tofu or
150g minced pork or chicken if you want to make
this soup more substantial.

Cutting daikon into thin slices

Cutting beans into 2cm pieces

salmon miso and shiitake soup

PREPARATION TIME 10 MINUTES • COOKING TIME 30 MINUTES

Straining the salmon stock

Gradually adding stock to miso

Ginger juice can be obtained by squeezing grated fresh green (that is, young) ginger into a sieve set over a bowl. A piece of ginger measuring approximately 10cm in length will yield 2 tablespoons of grated ginger; this amount of grated ginger should in turn yield the 2 teaspoons of juice used in this recipe.

1kg salmon bones and heads
1 small brown onion (80g), quartered
1.25 litres (5 cups) water
¹/₄ cup (60g) white miso (shiro miso)
4 shiitake mushrooms, sliced thinly
2 teaspoons fresh ginger juice
16 snow pea sprouts, trimmed into 4cm lengths
¹/₃ cup (80g) finely shredded daikon

1 Combine salmon bones and heads in large saucepan with onion and the water. Bring to a boil; reduce heat, simmer, uncovered, 20 minutes. Remove any scum from surface of stock. Strain stock mixture through muslin-lined strainer into large clean bowl. Return stock to same cleaned saucepan.

2 Place miso in small bowl, gradually add 1 cup (250ml) of the hot stock, stirring, until miso dissolves. Add to saucepan, stir to combine.

3 Add mushrooms, return to a simmer. Remove from heat; stir in ginger juice.

4 Divide soup among bowls; top with sprouts and daikon.

SERVES 4

tips For a stronger flavour, simmer the stock after straining to intensify its flavour.

You can use red miso. Red miso is stronger and saltier, so only use about 2 tablespoons in this recipe.

serving suggestion Serve with deep-fried tofu strips.

clear soup with tofu and wakame

PREPARATION TIME 15 MINUTES
COOKING TIME 10 MINUTES

Wakame is a highly nutritious seaweed which is practically black when purchased dried, but reconstitutes to a bright-green colour. The leaves are usually stripped from the central vein.

5g dried seaweed (wakame)
200g firm tofu, cut into 8 slices
1 litre (4 cups) primary dashi (see page 117)
1 tablespoon sake
2 teaspoons light soy sauce
1 teaspoon finely shredded lemon rind

1 Place seaweed in small bowl, cover with cold water; stand about 10 minutes or until softened. Drain; squeeze out excess water. Chop coarsely, removing any hard ribs.

2 Meanwhile, using a 3.5cm flower-shaped cutter, cut a flower from each tofu slice.

3 Divide seaweed and tofu among serving bowls.

4 Bring dashi to a boil in medium saucepan; stir in sake and sauce. Divide soup among serving bowls; sprinkle with lemon rind.

SERVES 4

tips If you don't own a flower cutter, cut tofu into 1.5cm cubes.

Use a citrus zester to make the long, very fine shreds of lemon rind.

Squeezing excess water from wakame

Cutting tofu into flower shapes

beef and rice soup

PREPARATION TIME 10 MINUTES • COOKING TIME 10 MINUTES

Cutting beef into
paper-thin slices

Arranging beef, seeds and
onion on top of the rice

*Koshihikari rice is grown locally from Japanese seed. If
necessary, you can substitute it with a medium-grain white rice.
White fish fillets can be used instead of beef, and shichimi
togarashi (seven-spice mix) or chilli can be used instead of the
wasabi. In Japan, green tea is sometimes used for the broth
instead of dashi. You will need 1¹/₂ cups (300g) uncooked rice
to make 4 cups (600g) cooked rice.*

1.25 litres (5 cups) primary dashi (see page 117)
3 teaspoons light soy sauce
4 cups (600g) hot cooked koshihikari rice
150g lean beef fillet, cut into paper-thin slices
2 teaspoons toasted white sesame seeds
2 green onions, chopped finely
1 tablespoon wasabi

1 Bring dashi and sauce to a boil in medium saucepan.

2 Divide hot rice among serving bowls; arrange beef,
   seeds and onion on top of the rice. Pour equal amounts
   of hot dashi mixture into bowls, taking care not to
   dislodge the arrangement; serve immediately with
   wasabi in individual dishes.

SERVES 4

tips If you place beef, wrapped in plastic wrap, in your
freezer for about an hour, it will be easier to slice thinly.

Beef will cook in the hot dashi mixture if sliced very
thinly. You can also brown unsliced beef in medium
non-stick frying pan to add extra flavour to soup.

Slitting underside of prawn

Pushing prawn tail through slit

Removing excess moisture
from cooked spinach

Making lemon-rind triangles

clear soup with prawns and spinach

PREPARATION TIME 20 MINUTES
COOKING TIME 15 MINUTES

4 medium uncooked prawns (100g)
50g baby spinach leaves
4 strips (1cm x 4cm) lemon rind
1 litre (4 cups) primary dashi (see page 117)
2 teaspoons light soy sauce

1 Shell and devein prawns, leaving tails intact. Slit
   underside of prawns; press flat. Cut small slit in
   centre of each prawn; push tail through slit.

2 Cook prawns in small saucepan of boiling water,
   uncovered, 1 minute or until just changed in colour;
   drain on absorbent paper.

3 Boil, steam or microwave spinach until just wilted.
   Rinse under cold water; drain well by laying spinach
   evenly across bamboo sushi mat, roll firmly, squeezing
   to remove excess moisture.

4 Starting at opposite ends of a rectangular strip of rind,
   cut slits along both long sides, not quite through to the
   other end; twist to form an open triangle. Repeat with
   remaining strips of rind.

5 Bring dashi to a boil in medium saucepan, add sauce.

6 Divide spinach and prawns, tails facing up, among
   serving bowls; divide soup among serving bowls, top
   with rind triangles.

SERVES 4

tip The method used to create the lemon-rind
triangles can also be used successfully with limes,
oranges, cucumber and carrot.

salmon miso and shiitake soup

PREPARATION TIME 10 MINUTES • COOKING TIME 30 MINUTES

Straining the salmon stock

Gradually adding stock to miso

Ginger juice can be obtained by squeezing grated fresh green (that is, young) ginger into a sieve set over a bowl. A piece of ginger measuring approximately 10cm in length will yield 2 tablespoons of grated ginger; this amount of grated ginger should in turn yield the 2 teaspoons of juice used in this recipe.

1kg salmon bones and heads
1 small brown onion (80g), quartered
1.25 litres (5 cups) water
¼ cup (60g) white miso (shiro miso)
4 shiitake mushrooms, sliced thinly
2 teaspoons fresh ginger juice
16 snow pea sprouts, trimmed into 4cm lengths
⅓ cup (80g) finely shredded daikon

1 Combine salmon bones and heads in large saucepan with onion and the water. Bring to a boil; reduce heat, simmer, uncovered, 20 minutes. Remove any scum from surface of stock. Strain stock mixture through muslin-lined strainer into large clean bowl. Return stock to same cleaned saucepan.

2 Place miso in small bowl, gradually add 1 cup (250ml) of the hot stock, stirring, until miso dissolves. Add to saucepan, stir to combine.

3 Add mushrooms, return to a simmer. Remove from heat; stir in ginger juice.

4 Divide soup among bowls; top with sprouts and daikon.

SERVES 4

tips For a stronger flavour, simmer the stock after straining to intensify its flavour.

You can use red miso. Red miso is stronger and saltier, so only use about 2 tablespoons in this recipe.

serving suggestion Serve with deep-fried tofu strips.

rice
& noodles

Cutting stems from reconstituted mushrooms

Pouring egg over chicken mixture

Finely chopping chives

chicken and egg on rice

oyako donburi

PREPARATION TIME 10 MINUTES (plus standing time)
COOKING TIME 10 MINUTES

Donburi refers to a bowl and also the rice combination which is served in it. Chicken and egg donburi is called oyako donburi in Japanese, meaning parent and child. Koshihikari rice is grown locally from Japanese seed. You can substitute a white medium-grain rice if it's unavailable. You will need 1 1/2 cups (300g) uncooked rice to make 4 cups (600g) hot cooked rice.

4 dried shiitake mushrooms
1/2 cup (125ml) secondary dashi (see page 117)
1/4 cup (60ml) japanese soy sauce
2 tablespoons mirin
1 teaspoon sugar
100g chicken breast fillet, sliced thinly
1 small leek (200g), sliced thinly
6 eggs, beaten lightly
4 cups (600g) hot cooked koshihikari rice
2 tablespoons finely chopped fresh chives

1 Place mushrooms in small heatproof bowl, cover with boiling water, stand about 20 minutes or until just tender; drain. Discard stems and halve caps.

2 Meanwhile, bring dashi, sauce, mirin and sugar to a boil in large frying pan.

3 Add chicken, leek and mushrooms; cook, covered, about 3 minutes or until chicken is tender.

4 Pour egg over chicken mixture; cook, covered, over low heat about 2 minutes or until egg just sets.

5 Divide rice among serving bowls; top with chicken mixture, sprinkle with chives.

SERVES 4

tip Egg mixture should be just set, still a little runny in areas. Remove from heat and keep covered to cook egg a little longer, if desired.

serving suggestion Serve with tempura prawns.

individual udon casserole

PREPARATION TIME 15 MINUTES (plus standing time) • COOKING TIME 20 MINUTES

Slicing carrot as thinly
as possible

Vegetables arranged over
noodles before adding broth

Using wooden spoon to make
a small hollow in noodles

Sliding egg into hollow
in noodles

*Udon are thick wheat noodles. Here, they form the basis of
individual casseroles which are cooked on the stove top in
donabes, earthenware flameproof pots. If donabes are not
available, cook in a flameproof dish and serve food at the table.*

400g dried thick udon
200g chicken breast fillet, chopped coarsely
2 teaspoons japanese soy sauce
2 teaspoons sake
250g spinach, trimmed
2^1/$_2$ cups (625ml) secondary dashi (see page 117)
2 tablespoons light soy sauce
1 tablespoon mirin
1 medium carrot (120g), sliced thinly
4 fresh shiitake mushrooms, sliced thinly
2 green onions, chopped coarsely
4 eggs
^{1}/$_4$ teaspoon seven-spice mix
(shichimi togarashi)

1 Cook noodles in large saucepan of boiling water,
   uncovered, until just tender; drain. Rinse under
   cold water, drain.

2 Combine chicken, japanese soy sauce and sake
   in small bowl; stand, covered, 10 minutes.

3 Boil, steam or microwave spinach until just
   wilted, rinse under cold water; squeeze out excess
   water, slice thickly.

4 Combine dashi, light soy sauce and mirin in medium
   saucepan, bring to a boil; keep warm.

5 Place ^{1}/$_2$ cup (125ml) of the broth in small saucepan,
   add carrot; cook 2 minutes. Add chicken; cook 2 minutes.
   Add mushrooms; cook about 1 minute longer or until chicken is tender.

6 Divide noodles between four 2^1/$_2$-cup (625ml) flameproof pots, arrange carrot,
   chicken, mushrooms, spinach and onion among pots. Cover with broth.

7 Cover pots, bring to a boil. Using the back of a spoon, make a small hollow
   in noodles; break eggs, one at a time, into small bowl, slide an egg into each
   hollow. Cover pots, remove from heat; stand, covered, until egg just sets.
   Just before serving, sprinkle each pot with a tiny pinch of seven-spice mix.

SERVES 4

tip Dried udon are available in different thicknesses; cooking times vary with
the size. Fresh udon are available from most supermarkets. There is no need to
refrigerate or cook them before use. Rinse under hot water before adding to pan.

serving suggestion Serve with thinly sliced fish cakes or tempura prawns.

Slicing beef thinly

Using chopsticks to separate noodles as they cook

Cutting cooked noodles into 10cm lengths

Adding onion and noodles to sweetened beef sauce

sweet soy beef on rice

PREPARATION TIME 10 MINUTES
COOKING TIME 10 MINUTES

Shirataki translates from Japanese as white waterfall, which rather romantically describes these transparent thin noodles which are sold fresh in water packs. They are made from the starchy tubers of konnyaku, which is also known as devil's tongue or elephant's foot. You will need 2 cups (400g) uncooked rice to make 5 cups (920g) hot cooked rice. The ginger juice is optional; you will need about 2 tablespoons grated fresh ginger to make 2 teaspoons ginger juice.

200g gelatinous noodles (shirataki), drained
$1/2$ cup (125ml) japanese soy sauce
1 tablespoon sugar
$1/4$ cup (60ml) mirin or sweet white wine
300g beef eye fillet, sliced paper thin
2 green onions, sliced diagonally into 2cm lengths
2 teaspoons fresh ginger juice (see page 38)
5 cups (920g) hot cooked koshihikari rice

1 Place noodles in medium saucepan of boiling water; bring to a boil. Cook 1 minute, separating noodles with chopsticks. Drain noodles, cut into 10cm lengths.

2 Bring sauce, sugar and mirin to a boil in medium saucepan. Add beef; cook, stirring, until beef just changes colour. Strain beef over medium heatproof bowl; return sauce to same saucepan.

3 Add onion and noodles to the pan and simmer about 3 minutes or until onion softens. Return beef to pan, add ginger juice; heat through.

4 Divide rice among serving bowls. Top rice with beef and noodles and about $1/4$ cup (60ml) of the sauce.

SERVES 4

tips Beef will be easier to slice if it's been placed in the freezer for about an hour before cutting.

You can substitute rice or cellophane noodles (harusame) for the shirataki.

chilled soba

Pouring dipping sauce into individual side dishes

Immersing noodles in iced water to chill

In summer, soba (buckwheat noodles) are served chilled on basket plates or bamboo boxes with slatted bases.

250g dried soba
³/₄ cup (180ml) primary dashi (see page 117)
2 tablespoons japanese soy sauce
2 tablespoons mirin
¹/₂ teaspoon sugar
2 green onions, chopped finely
1 teaspoon wasabi
¹/₂ toasted seaweed sheet (yaki-nori), sliced thinly

1 Cook noodles in large saucepan of boiling water, uncovered, until just tender; drain. Rinse under cold water; drain.

2 Heat dashi, sauce, mirin and sugar in small saucepan, stirring, until sugar dissolves; cool dipping sauce.

3 Divide dipping sauce, onion and wasabi among individual side dishes.

4 Just before serving, place noodles in a strainer and immerse in iced water to chill. Drain and divide among serving baskets or dishes; top with seaweed strips.

5 Add onion and wasabi to dipping sauce according to taste then dip noodles in sauce before eating.

SERVES 4

fried soba

PREPARATION TIME 15 MINUTES • COOKING TIME 20 MINUTES

Cutting onion into wedges

Shredding cabbage finely with a heavy sharp knife

Although more Chinese in origin, this is still a popular Japanese dish. Soba are noodles made from buckwheat and wheat flours. They are the first meal of the year for many Japanese, eaten at midnight to ensure good luck and health in the coming year. Ao-nori is a dried laver seaweed which grows on rocks in bays and at the mouths of rivers. It is sold in flakes for sprinkling as a garnish.

250g dried soba
1 tablespoon sesame oil
2 tablespoons vegetable oil
300g minced pork
1 medium brown onion (150g),
   cut into eight wedges
1 clove garlic, crushed
1 teaspoon grated fresh ginger
10 cups (500g) finely shredded cabbage
1 medium red capsicum (200g), sliced finely
2 tablespoons red pickled ginger (beni-shoga)
2 teaspoons shredded dried seaweed (ao-nori)

SAUCE
1 tablespoon sugar
1/4 cup (60ml) mirin
2 tablespoons sake
1/4 cup (60ml) japanese soy sauce

1 Cook noodles in large saucepan of boiling water, uncovered, until just tender, drain.

2 Heat sesame oil and 1 tablespoon of the vegetable oil in a wok or large frying pan, stir-fry pork over medium heat until browned lightly. Remove from wok, cover to keep warm.

3 In same wok, heat remaining vegetable oil; stir-fry onion, garlic and fresh ginger until onion softens. Add cabbage and capsicum, cook until tender. Add pickled ginger, pork, noodles and sauce, toss to combine and reheat. Serve sprinkled with seaweed.

sauce Heat combined ingredients in a small saucepan, stirring, until sugar dissolves.

SERVES 4

soba in broth

Slicing leek thinly on
the diagonal

*This was originally devised in the early 17th century as a
nutritious soup which could be prepared quickly for hurried
labourers and craftsmen. Shichimi togarashi is a mix of
seven spices, based on hot chillies.*

200g dried soba
3 cups (750ml) primary dashi (see page 117)
1/4 cup (60ml) japanese soy sauce
2 tablespoons mirin
1 teaspoon sugar
1 tablespoon vegetable oil
400g chicken breast fillet, sliced thinly
2 medium leeks (700g), sliced thinly
1/4 teaspoon seven-spice mix (shichimi togarashi)

Adding mirin to chicken and
leek mixture

1 Cook noodles in large saucepan of boiling water,
  uncovered, until just tender; drain, cover to keep warm.

2 Combine dashi, 2 tablespoons of the sauce, half of the
  mirin and half of the sugar in medium saucepan, bring
  to a boil; remove from heat, cover broth to keep hot.

3 Heat oil in medium frying pan; cook chicken and leek,
  stirring, until chicken is just cooked. Stir in remaining
  sauce, mirin and sugar; bring to a boil.

4 Divide noodles evenly among serving bowls, top with
  chicken mixture and cover with broth. Sprinkle with
  a tiny pinch of seven-spice mix.

SERVES 4

tip Add 1 tablespoon grated fresh ginger to the
broth for extra flavour.

tempura udon

PREPARATION TIME 20 MINUTES
COOKING TIME 10 MINUTES

For more information on preparing and cooking tempura, read the tips on page 97.

Scoring underside of prawns

320g dried thick udon
1 litre (4 cups) primary dashi (see page 117)
1/2 cup (125ml) japanese soy sauce
1/2 cup (125ml) mirin
8 large uncooked prawns (400g)
vegetable oil, for deep-frying
plain flour, for dusting
1/4 teaspoon seven-spice mix (shichimi togarashi)
2 green onions, chopped finely

TEMPURA BATTER
1/2 cup (75g) plain flour
1/2 cup (75g) cornflour
1 teaspoon baking powder
1 cup (250ml) iced soda water

Stirring soda water into batter

1 Cook noodles in large saucepan boiling water, uncovered, until just tender; drain.

2 Bring dashi, sauce and mirin to a boil in medium saucepan; reduce heat, simmer broth 10 minutes.

3 Meanwhile, shell and devein prawns, leaving tails intact. Score the underside of prawns to prevent curling during cooking.

Removing prawn from oil

4 Heat oil in small saucepan. Dip prawns, one at a time, in flour, shake off excess; dip in tempura batter. Deep-fry until browned lightly; drain on absorbent paper. Repeat until all prawns are cooked.

5 Just before serving, divide noodles among serving bowls, place two prawns on top of noodles, ladle broth over and sprinkle with seven-spice mix. Sprinkle with onion.

tempura batter Combine flours, baking powder and soda water in medium bowl. Do not overmix; mixture should be lumpy.

SERVES 4

tofu
& eggs

grilled tofu with sesame and spinach miso

PREPARATION TIME 10 MINUTES (plus standing time) • COOKING TIME 10 MINUTES

Pressing tofu between two chopping boards

Placing shreds of rind into iced water to make rind curl

Tofu is pressed to remove excess liquid before being deep-fried, pan-fried or pureed. Use lemon zester to make lemon rind curls for decoration.

600g firm tofu
$1/2$ cup (150g) white miso (shiro miso)
2 teaspoons sugar
2 tablespoons mirin
$1/3$ cup (80ml) primary dashi (see page 117)
2 tablespoons tahini
8 spinach leaves
1 tablespoon finely shredded lemon rind

1 Press tofu between two chopping boards with a weight on top, raise one end; stand 25 minutes.

2 Combine miso, sugar, mirin and dashi in small saucepan; cook, stirring, until sugar dissolves. Stir in tahini.

3 Boil, steam or microwave spinach until just wilted. Squeeze out excess liquid. Blend or process spinach with half of the miso mixture.

4 Cut tofu into 2cm slices, pat dry with absorbent paper; place on oiled oven tray, cook under hot grill about 3 minutes or until browned lightly. Spread spinach miso onto half of the tofu pieces; spread remaining tofu with remaining miso mixture. Cook under hot grill about 2 minutes or until miso is browned lightly. Sprinkle with rind before serving.

SERVES 4

tips Rind can be soaked in iced water to make it curl. Misos can vary in strength, so adjust sugar to taste.
serving suggestion If you wish to cut the tofu into bite-sized pieces, use Japanese bamboo forks to serve.

steamed custard

chawan-mushi

PREPARATION TIME 20 MINUTES (plus standing time) • COOKING TIME 15 MINUTES

Deveining the shelled prawns with a toothpick

4 medium uncooked prawns (100g)
3 teaspoons japanese soy sauce
1 teaspoon sake
75g chicken breast fillet, sliced thinly
1³/4 cups (430ml) cold primary dashi (see page 117)
1 tablespoon sake, extra
4 eggs, beaten lightly
4 fresh shiitake mushrooms,
  stems removed, quartered
1/2 small carrot (35g), halved, sliced thinly
8 spinach leaves, blanched, chopped coarsely
1 tablespoon finely shredded lemon rind

Straining egg mixture through cloth-lined sieve

1 Shell and devein prawns, leaving tails intact. Remove vein by inserting a toothpick under the vein in the centre back and gently pulling vein out. Combine 1 teaspoon of the sauce and sake in medium bowl, add chicken, mix well, cover; stand 10 minutes.

2 Combine dashi, remaining sauce and extra sake in medium bowl; stir egg in gently. Strain egg mixture through fine or cloth-lined sieve into large jug.

Pouring egg mixture into cups

3 Divide chicken, prawns and vegetables between four ³/4-cup (180ml) tea or coffee cups; divide egg mixture among cups, leaving 1cm space between egg mixture and top of cup. Cover cups with plastic wrap.

4 Place cups inside a large bamboo steamer, allowing space between cups for the steam to circulate. Place steamer over wok or large saucepan of simmering water, reduce heat; steam, covered, about 20 minutes or until custard sets.

5 Remove plastic wrap then place hot cups on saucers or small plates; sprinkle tops with lemon rind.

SERVES 4

tips Individual soufflé dishes or ramekins can be used if you don't have small tea or coffee cups.

To blanch spinach, place leaves in a medium heatproof bowl, cover with boiling water, stand 1 minute; drain, squeeze spinach to remove excess moisture.

Placing cups in steamer

deep-fried tofu in broth

age-dashi dofu

PREPARATION TIME 15 MINUTES (plus standing time) • COOKING TIME 15 MINUTES

Coating tofu in cornflour

Age-dashi dofu is the most classic of tofu dishes, simply deep-fried tofu with a dashi-based sauce and garnishes. Tofu should be pressed before being deep-fried, pan-fried or pureed, to remove excess liquid.

300g firm tofu
2 tablespoons cornflour
vegetable oil, for deep-frying
3/4 cup (180ml) primary dashi (see page 117)
2 tablespoons japanese soy sauce
2 tablespoons mirin
2 tablespoons finely grated daikon
1 tablespoon grated fresh ginger
1 green onion, chopped finely
2 teaspoons smoked dried bonito flakes (katsuobushi)

1 Press tofu between two chopping boards with a weight on top, raise one end; stand 25 minutes.

2 Cut tofu into eight even-sized pieces; pat dry between layers of absorbent paper. Toss in cornflour, shake away excess cornflour. Heat oil in medium saucepan or deep-fryer; cook tofu, in batches, until browned lightly all over. Drain on absorbent paper.

3 Combine dashi, sauce and mirin in small saucepan; bring to a boil.

4 Place two pieces of tofu in each serving bowl; divide daikon, ginger and onion among bowls, pour over dashi mixture. Top with bonito flakes.

SERVES 4

tip Instead of serving tofu with accompaniments, try seasoning cornflour with chilli flakes or sesame seeds.

Deep-frying tofu

thick omelette

PREPARATION TIME 5 MINUTES • COOKING TIME 10 MINUTES (plus cooling time)

Folding omelette in three

Lifting cooked omelette to allow mixture to spread underneath

Wrapping finished omelette in bamboo mat

To give the omelette a colourful centre, wrap the first omelette around cooked carrot and green onion. Or add a toasted seaweed sheet (yaki-nori) between each layer of egg. You will need a piece of daikon about 3cm long and 5cm in diameter to make the accompaniment for this recipe.

8 eggs, beaten lightly
1 tablespoon water or secondary dashi (see page 117)
2 teaspoons sugar
3 teaspoons mirin
2 teaspoons light soy sauce
2 tablespoons vegetable oil
¹/₃ cup (80ml) japanese soy sauce
¹/₄ cup (60g) finely grated daikon, drained well

1 Combine egg, the water, sugar, mirin and light soy sauce in a large jug. Stir until sugar dissolves.

2 Oil base of traditional square frying pan or medium (about 20cm) frying pan with a little of the vegetable oil; place over low to medium heat.

3 Pour in enough egg mixture to just cover base of pan; cook, tilting pan to spread mixture evenly. Break any large air bubbles so the omelette lies flat. When the mixture is almost set, run chopsticks or spatula around edge of pan to loosen omelette.

4 Starting from the back of the pan, fold omelette into three towards the front of the pan. Gently push folded omelette to the back of the pan.

5 Lightly oil pan again, repeat procedure, lifting up the cooked omelette so the egg mixture runs underneath it. When nearly cooked, fold in three, starting with the omelette already cooked and folded. Repeat this step until all mixture is used.

6 Tip omelette onto a bamboo mat and wrap firmly to form a compact rectangle. Cool omelette; cut into 1cm slices. Serve with japanese soy sauce and daikon.

SERVES 4

tip Sliced omelette can also be used for nigiri-zushi (raw-fish-topped sushi) or cut lengthways into long, thin strips and used as a filling for sushi rolls.

savoury pancake

okonomi-yaki

Adding combined dashi and egg to dry ingredients

Slicing cabbage thinly

Brushing pancake with japanese worcestershire sauce

PREPARATION TIME 10 MINUTES (plus standing time)
COOKING TIME 10 MINUTES

Okonomi means "your choice" since these pancakes are usually prepared to order with a choice of fillings so each diner can suit his or her taste. It's important not to leave the batter standing too long or it will become sticky. Ao-nori is made from laver seaweed which grows on rocks in bays and at the mouths of rivers. It is sold dried in flakes for sprinkling as a garnish. Beni-shoga is finely sliced or shredded pickled ginger which is deep red in colour. Bonito is an oily fish which, when dried and flaked, is widely used in the Japanese kitchen.

2 cups (300g) plain flour
$1^1/_2$ teaspoons baking powder
$1^1/_2$ cups (375ml) secondary dashi (see page 117)
1 egg, beaten lightly
2 large cabbage leaves
125g minced pork
2 tablespoons vegetable oil
$^1/_2$ cup (125ml) japanese worcestershire sauce
2 tablespoons red pickled ginger (beni-shoga)
1 tablespoon shredded dried seaweed (ao-nori)
$^1/_4$ cup (3g) smoked dried bonito flakes (katsuobushi)

1   Sift flour and baking powder together in medium bowl. Gradually add combined dashi and egg, mixing quickly until smooth; do not overmix. Cover; stand 30 minutes.

2   Remove thick ribs from cabbage leaves and discard; slice remaining leaves thinly. Add cabbage and pork to batter; mix gently.

3   Heat a quarter of the oil in medium frying pan over low heat. Spoon in a quarter of the batter and flatten with a spatula. When bubbles begin to appear in mixture, turn over and brush cooked side with sauce. Turn pancake over again and brush other side with sauce. Quickly repeat once more, so the sauce caramelises onto the pancake. Remove from pan, cover; keep warm. Repeat with remaining oil and batter.

3   Serve pancakes sprinkled with pickled ginger, seaweed and bonito flakes.

SERVES 4

tips Japanese worcestershire sauce comes in different strengths; most are milder than western worcestershire so adjust the amount added according to taste. Commercial or homemade tonkatsu sauce (see page 76) makes a good substitute.
Okonomi-yaki packet mixes are available from Asian stores, either plain or with octopus.
serving suggestion Chopped octopus is a particular favourite in this dish in Japan.

fried tofu with daikon and ginger

PREPARATION TIME 10 MINUTES (plus standing time) • COOKING TIME 10 MINUTES

Coating tofu in sesame seeds

Cooking tofu in vegetable oil

You will need a piece of daikon about 6cm long and 5cm in diameter to make the accompaniment for this recipe.

600g firm tofu
$1/3$ cup (50g) plain flour
2 eggs, beaten lightly
$1/3$ cup (50g) black sesame seeds
$1/3$ cup (50g) white sesame seeds
vegetable oil, for deep-frying
$1/2$ cup (120g) finely grated daikon, drained well
2 teaspoons grated fresh ginger

SAUCE
$1/3$ cup (80ml) primary dashi (see page 117)
1 teaspoon mirin
1 tablespoon japanese soy sauce

1 Press tofu between two chopping boards with a weight on top, raise one end; stand 25 minutes.

2 Cut tofu into 2.5cm cubes; toss in flour, shake off excess flour. Dip tofu in egg, then in combined seeds to coat.

3 Heat oil in medium saucepan or deep-fryer; cook tofu, in batches, until browned lightly all over, drain on absorbent paper or wire rack. Serve with warmed sauce and daikon topped with ginger.

sauce Heat combined ingredients in small saucepan.

SERVES 4

tips If you like, you can add dried smoked bonito flakes to the sesame seeds.

Coat tofu with breadcrumbs instead of sesame seeds, if preferred.

meat
poultry & seafood

crumbed pork
tonkatsu

PREPARATION TIME 15 MINUTES (plus soaking time) • COOKING TIME 15 MINUTES

Dipping pork in breadcrumbs

Deep-frying pork

Tonkatsu is a rich, fruity barbecue sauce that can be made at home or purchased in Asian stores. Available in two crumb sizes, japanese breadcrumbs are light and crunchy; use either size. You'll need a quarter of a small cabbage for this recipe.

4 pork steaks (600g)
1/4 cup (35g) plain flour
2 eggs, beaten lightly
2 teaspoons water
2 cups (100g) dried japanese breadcrumbs
6 cups (300g) finely shredded cabbage
vegetable oil, for deep-frying
1 lemon, cut into wedges
3 teaspoons japanese mustard

TONKATSU SAUCE
2 tablespoons japanese worcestershire sauce
1/3 cup (80ml) tomato sauce
1 teaspoon japanese soy sauce
2 tablespoons sake
1 teaspoon japanese mustard

1 Pound pork gently with a meat mallet. Toss in flour, shaking off excess flour.

2 Dip pork in combined egg and water, then in breadcrumbs to coat.

3 Soak cabbage in iced water for 5 minutes to crisp; drain.

4 Heat enough oil to cover pork in medium saucepan or deep-fryer. Add pork and cook, in batches, turning occasionally, 5 minutes or until golden brown both sides. Skim oil during cooking to remove any crumbs.

5 Drain pork on absorbent paper and cut diagonally into 2cm slices. Place cabbage on serving plate and arrange pork against cabbage so it appears uncut. Serve with lemon wedges, mustard and tonkatsu sauce.

tonkatsu sauce Combine ingredients in small saucepan, bring to a boil; whisk. Remove from heat; cool.

SERVES 4

pan-fried dumplings

gyoza

PREPARATION TIME 20 MINUTES (plus refrigeration time)
COOKING TIME 10 MINUTES

Pleating damp side of wrapper

Pinching both sides of
dumpling together

Removing dumplings from pan

*You can vary the filling of these dumplings by adding chopped
prawns, cheese, capsicum or scrambled egg. You'll need about
a quarter of a medium cabbage to make this recipe.*

300g minced pork
2 tablespoons japanese soy sauce
1/4 teaspoon white pepper
1 teaspoon sugar
1 tablespoon sake
1 egg, beaten lightly
2 teaspoons sesame oil
6 1/2 cups (325g) finely chopped cabbage
4 green onions, chopped finely
50 gyoza or gow gee wrappers
1 tablespoon vegetable oil

1 Mix pork, sauce, pepper, sugar, sake, egg, sesame oil,
   cabbage and onion in medium bowl. Refrigerate 1 hour.

2 Take a wrapper and wet the edge of one side. Place a
   rounded teaspoon of pork mixture in centre of wrapper
   and pleat the damp side of wrapper only. Pinch both
   sides together to seal. Repeat with remaining wrappers
   and pork mixture.

3 Cover base of large frying pan with water, bring to
   a boil. Add dumplings, in batches; reduce heat and
   simmer, covered, 3 minutes. Remove dumplings from
   pan with slotted spoon, drain and dry pan.

4 Heat oil in same frying pan; cook dumplings, uncovered,
   in batches, unpleated side and base only, until golden.

MAKES 50

serving suggestion Serve with soy sauce mixed with
chilli oil, or rice vinegar or ponzu sauce (see page 88).

78

Cutting pork into strips

Removing ribs from cabbage

sauteed pork and ginger cabbage

PREPARATION TIME 15 MINUTES (plus marinating time)
COOKING TIME 10 MINUTES

Ginger juice is made by squeezing grated fresh green (that is, young) ginger into a sieve set over a bowl. A piece of ginger approximately 15cm long will yield 3 tablespoons of grated ginger; this amount of grated ginger should in turn yield the 3 teaspoons of juice used in this recipe.

1 teaspoon sugar
2 tablespoons sake
1/4 cup (60ml) japanese soy sauce
1 teaspoon grated fresh ginger
400g pork fillet
8 chinese cabbage leaves
2 tablespoons vegetable oil
3 teaspoons fresh ginger juice

1 Combine sugar, sake, sauce and grated ginger in medium bowl; stir until sugar dissolves.

2 Cut pork into 5cm lengths, cut each piece into thin strips. Add pork to marinade; stand 10 minutes. (If marinated longer than 10 minutes, pork will become tough.) Drain pork over small bowl; reserve marinade.

3 Meanwhile, remove thick ribs from cabbage, cut leaves into 4cm squares.

4 Heat oil in large frying pan or wok; stir-fry pork 3 minutes. Add cabbage, reserved marinade and ginger juice; stir-fry until hot. Serve with steamed rice.

SERVES 4

yakitori

seasoned chicken on skewers

PREPARATION TIME 20 MINUTES • COOKING TIME 15 MINUTES (plus cooling time)

Soaking bamboo skewers

Threading chicken and vegetables onto skewers

Brushing skewers with sauce during cooking

Chicken wings, chicken liver or vegetables of your choice can be used in this dish, but remember to cut even-sized pieces and use ingredients that take about the same time to cook. You will need to soak eight bamboo skewers in water for an hour to prevent them from splintering and scorching.

500g chicken thigh or breast fillets,
    cut into 2.5cm pieces
1 medium red capsicum (200g), chopped coarsely
4 fresh shiitake mushrooms, stems removed, halved
6 thick green onions, trimmed, cut into 2.5cm lengths
1/4 teaspoon japanese pepper (sansho powder)

SAUCE
1/2 cup (125ml) japanese soy sauce
1/2 cup (125ml) sake
1/4 cup (60ml) mirin
2 tablespoons sugar

1 Thread chicken and vegetables onto eight bamboo skewers, leaving space between pieces to allow even cooking.

2 Cook, in batches, on heated oiled grill plate (or grill or barbecue), turning and brushing with sauce occasionally, until browned all over and cooked through.

3 Serve yakitori sprinkled with japanese pepper.

sauce Combine ingredients in small saucepan; bring to a boil. Reduce heat; simmer, uncovered, over medium heat until sauce reduces by a third, cool.

SERVES 4

tips Bottled yakitori sauce is readily available from Asian grocery stores.

The sauce can be used as a marinade for the chicken before cooking, but cook chicken on medium heat so marinade does not burn before meat cooks through.

You can substitute seven-spice mix (shichimi togarashi) for japanese pepper (sansho powder).

salmon teriyaki

PREPARATION TIME 10 MINUTES (plus standing time) • COOKING TIME 10 MINUTES

Shredding the daikon
using a mandoline

Turning salmon in marinade

Daikon is a large white radish with a sweet, fresh taste. In Japan it is often served, grated raw, as an accompaniment.

4 salmon fillets (700g), skinned
1/2 cup (120g) finely shredded daikon

TERIYAKI MARINADE
2/3 cup (160ml) japanese soy sauce
2/3 cup (160ml) mirin
2 tablespoons sake
1 tablespoon sugar

1 Place salmon in teriyaki marinade for 10 minutes, turning occasionally. Drain salmon over medium bowl; reserve marinade.

2 Soak daikon in small bowl of iced water for 15 minutes; drain well.

3 Cook salmon on heated oiled grill plate (or grill or barbecue), brushing occasionally with marinade, until cooked as desired. Bring reserved marinade to a boil in small saucepan. Reduce heat; simmer 5 minutes or until sauce thickens slightly.

4 Serve salmon with daikon, drizzle with sauce.

teriyaki marinade Combine ingredients in medium bowl; stir until sugar dissolves.

SERVES 4

tip Bought teriyaki sauce may be used, but it's stronger than homemade. Dilute it with mirin, sake or water.

beef and vegetable rolls

PREPARATION TIME 15 MINUTES • COOKING TIME 15 MINUTES (plus cooling time)

Slicing carrot into strips with
vegetable peeler

Blanching asparagus in
boiling water

Securing rolls with toothpicks

Adding sauce ingredients to pan

*To make larger rolls, use two or three slices of meat,
slightly overlapping. You could use rib eye steak (scotch fillet)
instead of the beef eye fillet.*

> 2 medium carrots (240g)
> 6 asparagus spears, halved lengthways
> 3 green onions
> 12 thin slices beef eye fillet (300g)
> 2 tablespoons cornflour
> 1 tablespoon vegetable oil
> 1 tablespoon sugar
> 1/4 cup (60ml) mirin or sweet rice wine
> 2 tablespoons sake
> 1/4 cup (60ml) japanese soy sauce

1 Using a vegetable peeler, slice carrot lengthways into
thin strips. Cut carrot strips to width of beef. Place
asparagus in heatproof bowl, cover with boiling water,
stand 2 minutes; drain, rinse under cold water, drain.
Cut asparagus and onions to width of beef.

2 Lay beef slices flat and sift 1 tablespoon of the
cornflour lightly over top. Lay two pieces each of
carrot and onion and one piece of asparagus across the
dusted side of each slice of beef and roll up. Tie rolls
with kitchen string or secure ends with toothpicks.
Dust rolls lightly with remaining cornflour.

3 Heat oil in medium frying pan and cook rolls until
lightly browned all over. Remove rolls from pan, wipe
oil from pan with absorbent paper; return rolls to pan.
Add combined sugar, mirin, sake and sauce; bring to a
boil. Reduce heat; simmer, turning occasionally, until
rolls are cooked through. If a thicker sauce is preferred,
remove rolls and boil sauce to reduce. Return rolls to
pan and coat with sauce.

4 Remove rolls from pan, cool 2 minutes. Remove and
discard toothpicks; cut rolls in half. Arrange on serving
plate and serve with remaining sauce.

SERVES 4

tips Very thinly sliced beef, sold as yakiniku or sukiyaki
beef, is available from Asian grocery stores.

Pork fillet can be used in this recipe instead of
beef eye fillet, if preferred.

seared beef

PREPARATION TIME 10 MINUTES (plus standing time) • COOKING TIME 8 MINUTES

Cooking beef on grill plate

Plunging beef into cold water

Slicing beef thinly

You can substitute rib eye (scotch fillet) or rump steak for the eye fillet. The beef in this recipe is raw in the middle. You'll need a piece of daikon about 10cm long and 5cm in diameter for this recipe.

1 cup (240g) finely shredded daikon
400g beef eye fillet
2 teaspoons vegetable oil
1 lebanese cucumber (130g), halved lengthways

PONZU SAUCE
¼ cup (60ml) lemon juice
¼ cup (60ml) japanese soy sauce
¼ cup (60ml) water or primary dashi
    (see page 117)
2 green onions, sliced thinly

1 Place daikon in medium bowl, cover with cold water, stand 15 minutes; drain.

2 Brush beef with oil and cook on heated oiled grill plate (or grill or barbecue) until browned all over. Allow to cool or plunge into cold water to stop cooking immediately. Drain and pat dry with absorbent paper.

3 Remove and discard seeds from cucumber; slice thinly. Cut beef into thin slices and arrange on a plate with mounds of daikon and cucumber. Serve with ponzu sauce.

ponzu sauce Combine juice, sauce and the water in small bowl; sprinkle with onion.

SERVES 4

serving suggestion Serve with separate bowls of finely chopped garlic, grated fresh ginger, lemon wedges and japanese soy sauce.

one-pot cooking

mixed one-pot dish

yosenabe

PREPARATION TIME 20 MINUTES (plus standing time)
COOKING TIME 10 MINUTES

Soaking dried cellophane noodles to reconstitute

Removing beards from mussels

Use some or all of the ingredients listed for this recipe, according to individual tastes. Harusame (cellophane noodles) are made from mung bean or potato starch.

30g dried cellophane noodles (harusame)
8 fresh shiitake mushrooms
8 uncooked medium prawns (200g)
8 medium mussels (200g)
300g firm tofu, pressed (see page 64)
200g chicken breast fillets, cut into 5cm pieces
200g pork fillet, sliced thinly
200g firm white fish fillets, cut into 5cm pieces
8 medium oysters
8 scallops
2 medium carrots (240g), sliced thinly lengthways
2 medium leeks (700g), sliced thickly
4 chinese cabbage leaves, chopped coarsely
1 litre (4 cups) secondary dashi (see page 117)
2 tablespoons japanese soy sauce
2 tablespoons mirin
2 tablespoons sake
4 green onions, chopped finely
1/2 cup (120g) red maple radish (momiji oroshi, see page 92), or finely grated daikon, drained well
1 quantity ponzu sauce (see page 88)

1   Place noodles in medium heatproof bowl, cover with boiling water, stand until just tender; drain.

2   Remove and discard mushroom stems; cut a cross in the top of caps. Shell and devein prawns, leaving tails intact. Remove fibrous mussel beards by pulling firmly. Cut tofu into 2cm cubes.

3   Arrange meats, seafood, vegetables and tofu on a large platter.

4   Bring dashi, sauce, mirin and sake to a boil in large flameproof casserole dish on a portable cooker, or in an electric frying pan, at the table.

5   Add a selection of ingredients to the broth and simmer until just cooked. Repeat with remaining ingredients. Add extra dashi or water if needed. Serve with individual serving bowls of onion, and mounded red maple radish in ponzu sauce.

SERVES 4

tips When vegetables and meat are eaten, the broth can be served with rice or extra noodles.

Drained fresh gelatinous noodles (shirataki) can be substituted for the cellophane noodles (harusame).

shabu-shabu

meat and vegetable one-pot with dipping sauces

PREPARATION TIME 20 MINUTES • COOKING TIME 10 MINUTES

Shabu-shabu is meant to be the sound of the paper-thin meat as it is gently swished with chopsticks through the hot broth, cooking in only a few seconds. It is cooked at the table in a flameproof dish or hotpot set on a portable gas or electric hot plate. Small portable cookers are readily available at Asian grocery stores. If you don't have one, you could use an electric frypan. When all meat and vegetables are eaten, the broth can be served with extra noodles or rice. Momiji oroshi (red maple radish) is said to resemble autumn maple leaves.

400g gelatinous noodles (shirataki), drained
12 fresh shiitake mushrooms
600g beef eye fillet, sliced thinly
300g firm tofu, pressed (see page 64), cut into 2cm cubes
4 leeks, halved lengthways, washed, sliced diagonally into 2cm pieces
6 chinese cabbage leaves, chopped coarsely
100g bamboo shoots, sliced finely
12 small pieces decorative wheat gluten (fu)
1 quantity ponzu sauce (see page 88)
$1/2$ cup (120g) red maple radish (momiji oroshi, see below),
    or finely grated daikon, drained well
4 green onions, chopped finely
10cm-long piece dried kelp (konbu), cut into 4 pieces
1.5 litres (6 cups) water or secondary dashi (see page 117)

RED MAPLE RADISH (MOMIJI OROSHI)
6cm-long 5cm-diameter piece daikon (120g), peeled
4 hot dried red chillies

1 Rinse noodles under hot water, drain. Cut into 20cm lengths.

2 Remove and discard mushroom stems; cut a cross in the top of caps. Arrange beef, tofu, vegetables and decorative wheat gluten on a platter.

3 Divide ponzu sauce, red maple radish and onion among individual serving bowls.

4 Make a few cuts along the edges of kelp to release the flavour. Place in a 2-litre (8 cup) flameproof casserole dish or pot with 1.125 litres ($4^1/2$ cups) of the water or dashi and bring to a boil. Remove kelp just before the water boils; reduce heat and simmer 4 minutes.

5 Add a selection of ingredients to the broth. As soon as they are cooked, remove and dip meat and vegetables in ponzu sauce. Add more ingredients and remaining water or dashi as required. Skim the surface of broth periodically to remove scum.

red maple radish (momiji oroshi) Using a chopstick, poke four holes in one end of daikon. Seed chillies and insert one into each hole with chopstick. Grate the daikon and chillies in a circular motion with a Japanese or fine-toothed grater. Squeeze out excess liquid. Shape into small mounds and place in individual serving dishes or in the centre of ponzu sauce.

SERVES 4

Cutting crosses in shiitake mushroom caps

Using chopstick to insert chilli in daikon for red maple radish

Cutting edges of kelp (konbu) to release flavour

Adding ingredients to broth

sukiyaki

meat and vegetable one-pot with sweet soy sauce

PREPARATION TIME 20 MINUTES • COOKING TIME 10 MINUTES

Slicing beef thinly

Greasing pan with beef fat

A traditional sukiyaki pan can be purchased from Japanese stores, however an electric frying pan is a good substitute. You could use beef sirloin, or rib eye (scotch fillet) instead of the rump. Small quantities of sukiyaki are cooked and served individually to guests. Each guest usually has a small bowl containing an egg which has been lightly beaten with chopsticks; the hot food is dipped into the egg before eating. The heat partly cooks the egg.

400g fresh gelatinous noodles (shirataki), drained
8 fresh shiitake mushrooms
600g beef rump steak
4 green onions, chopped finely
300g spinach, trimmed, chopped coarsely
125g can bamboo shoots, drained
200g firm tofu, pressed (see page 64),
    cut into 2cm cubes
4 eggs

BROTH

1 cup (250ml) japanese soy sauce
1/2 cup (125ml) sake
1/2 cup (125ml) mirin
1/2 cup (125ml) water
1/2 cup (110g) caster sugar

1 Rinse noodles under hot water, drain. Cut noodles into 15cm lengths.

2 Remove and discard mushroom stems; cut a cross in the top of caps.

3 Trim beef of all fat; slice thinly. Retain a small piece of beef fat for greasing the sukiyaki pan. Arrange ingredients on platters or in bowls. Place broth in medium bowl. Break eggs into individual bowls; beat lightly.

4 Heat greased sukiyaki pan (or electric frying pan) on a portable gas cooker at the table; add quarter of the beef, stir-fry until partly cooked. Add a quarter each of the vegetables, tofu, noodles and broth. Dip cooked ingredients in egg before eating.

5 As ingredients and broth are eaten, add remaining ingredients and broth to pan, in batches.

   broth Combine ingredients in a medium saucepan; cook over medium heat, stirring, until sugar dissolves.

SERVES 4

tip Sukiyaki beef is available fresh and frozen from Asian grocery stores and selected supermarkets.

vegetable tempura

PREPARATION TIME 20 MINUTES • COOKING TIME 20 MINUTES

Adjust the size or thickness of slower-cooking vegetables (such as sweet potato and pumpkin) to ensure they cook at the same rate as faster-cooking vegetables (such as mushrooms). Always use fresh, clean oil and keep at a constant temperature during cooking. Optimum temperature for vegetables is fairly hot, about 170ºC, and for seafood slightly higher; seafood is usually cooked after vegetables. For advice on deep-frying, see tips opposite.

1 medium brown onion (150g)
1 small fresh or frozen lotus root (200g)
8 fresh shiitake mushrooms
2 sheets toasted seaweed (yaki-nori)
20g cellophane noodles (harusame),
   cut in half
vegetable oil, for deep-frying
plain flour, for dusting ingredients
120g pumpkin, sliced thinly
50g green beans, halved
1 small kumara (250g), sliced thinly
1 baby eggplant (60g), sliced thinly
1 small red capsicum (150g), seeded,
   cut in squares
1 medium carrot (120g),
   sliced thinly, diagonally
250g firm tofu, pressed (see page 64),
   cut into 2cm cubes
1 lemon, cut into wedges

BATTER
1 egg, beaten lightly
2 cups (500ml) iced soda water
1 cup (150g) plain flour
1 cup (150g) cornflour

DIPPING SAUCE
1 cup (250ml) primary dashi
   (see page 117)
1/3 cup (80ml) mirin
1/3 cup (80ml) light soy sauce
1/2 cup (120g) finely grated daikon,
   drained well
3 teaspoons grated fresh ginger

1 Halve onion from root end. Insert toothpicks at regular intervals to hold onion rings together and slice in between (see page 99).

2 Peel lotus root and slice. Place in water with a dash of vinegar to prevent browning. If using canned lotus, drain and slice. Remove and discard mushroom stems; cut a cross in the top of caps.

3 Cut one sheet seaweed into 5cm squares, halve the other sheet and cut into 2cm-wide strips. Brush seaweed strips with water and wrap tightly around about 10 noodles, either at one end or in the middle; reserve noodle bunches.

4 Heat oil to moderately hot (170ºC). Dust ingredients, except seaweed squares, lightly in flour; shake off excess flour. Dip seaweed squares and other ingredients in batter, drain excess batter; deep-fry ingredients, in batches, until golden. Drain on absorbent paper. Only fry small amounts at a time and make sure enough time is allowed for oil to come back to correct temperature before adding next batch.

5 Finally, deep-fry reserved noodle bundles and serve as a garnish.

6 Serve immediately with lemon wedges and individual bowls of warm dipping sauce.

batter Combine egg in a bowl with iced water. Add sifted flours all at once, mixing lightly until just combined, but still very lumpy.

dipping sauce Combine dashi, mirin and sauce in medium saucepan and heat gently. Divide among four individual serving bowls. Shape daikon into four pyramid shapes. Place a pyramid in each serving bowl; top with even amounts of ginger.

SERVES 4

tips Make the batter just before beginning to deep-fry. It should never be mixed well, should not be smooth but should have lumps of dry flour through it with a ring of flour around the edges of the bowl. Always use iced or chilled water to make batter. For a thinner, lacier batter, add slightly more water. The batter should never stand for any length of time or it will become too heavy. It is preferable to make two smaller batches to avoid this happening.

Use absorbent paper to dry all of the foods to be coated. Lightly dust ingredients with flour to help the batter stick. Dip in batter and gently shake over the bowl to remove any excess. Pieces of seaweed are never floured and only battered on one side or flavour and texture is lost.

Sauce should be served warm for tempura so it does not cool the light and delicate coating on ingredients. Bottled tempura sauce is available from Asian grocery stores. It is usually concentrated and should be diluted with water.

To test if oil is the correct temperature, drop a small amount of batter into oil. If it drops just below the surface then bounces back, the oil is ready. If it drops to the bottom and slowly rises, the oil is not hot enough. If the batter skims across the surface, the oil is too hot and the batter will brown without the food cooking through. To bring the temperature down quickly, add a little extra oil. Clean the oil often during cooking to remove any leftover batter.

seafood tempura

PREPARATION TIME 20 MINUTES • COOKING TIME 20 MINUTES

Yaki-nori are toasted sheets of seaweed most commonly used for sushi or wrapping mouthfuls of breakfast rice. Here, they're used to secure bundles of noodles, and dipped in batter for tempura.

12 medium uncooked prawns (300g)
2 cleaned squid (180g)
2 medium brown onions (300g)
8 fresh shiitake or large button mushrooms
2 sheets toasted seaweed (yaki-nori)
20g dried wheat noodles (somen), cut in half
vegetable oil, for deep-frying
12 scallops
300g thin white fish fillets, cut into 3cm cubes
1 small red capsicum (150g), seeded, cut in 3cm squares
plain flour, for dusting ingredients
1 quantity batter (see page 96)
1 lemon, cut into wedges
1 quantity dipping sauce (see page 96)

1 Shell and devein prawns, leaving tails intact. Make three small cuts on the underside of each prawn, halfway through flesh, to prevent curling when cooked. Trim a thin edge off each tail and, with the back of a knife, gently press to expel any moisture that might make the oil spit during cooking.

2 Cut squid in half lengthways; lay flat, with shiny smooth-side up, on chopping board. Holding knife at 45-degree angle, slice diagonally halfway through flesh. Repeat, slicing in the opposite direction to make a diamond pattern. Cut squid into large squares or strips.

3 Halve onions from root end. Insert toothpicks at regular intervals to hold onion rings together and slice in between. Discard mushroom stems; cut a cross in the top of caps.

4 Cut one sheet seaweed into 5cm squares, halve the other sheet and cut into 2cm-wide strips. Brush seaweed strips with water and wrap tightly around about 10 noodles, either at one end or in the middle; reserve noodle bunches.

5 Heat oil to moderately hot (170°C). Dust seafood and vegetable ingredients, except seaweed squares, lightly in flour; shake off excess flour. Dip seaweed squares and other ingredients in batter, drain excess; deep-fry ingredients, in batches, until golden. Drain on absorbent paper. Only fry small amounts at a time and make sure enough time is allowed for oil to come back to correct temperature before adding next batch.

6 Finally, deep-fry reserved noodle bundles and serve as a garnish. Serve with lemon and bowls of dipping sauce.

SERVES 4

tip For decorative effect, secure strips of seaweed around prawn tails before deep-frying.

Cutting underside of prawns
to prevent curling

Trimming thin edge of each tail
and expelling any moisture

Slicing onion with toothpicks
inserted to hold rings together

Wrapping noodle bundles
with seaweed

mixed barbecue

teppanyaki

PREPARATION TIME 20 MINUTES (plus marinating time)
COOKING TIME 20 MINUTES

Although the flavours in the marinade and sauce are more suited to the Korean barbecue dish, bulgogi, they are becoming increasingly popular in Japan. You could substitute beef rump or sirloin steak for the eye fillet. Teppanyaki is traditionally cooked on a grill plate, on or near the table, and is eaten in batches; a portable electric grill is ideal. The method for this recipe, however, instructs you to cook the ingredients on the stove top; this is because most households don't own a portable grill.

Using a toothpick to
devein prawns

Adding prawns, chicken and
beef to marinade

4 large uncooked prawns (200g)
2 cloves garlic, crushed
1/4 cup (60ml) japanese soy sauce
1 small red chilli, seeded, chopped finely
350g chicken breast fillet, skin on, cut into 5cm pieces
500g beef eye fillet, sliced thinly
4 fresh shiitake mushrooms
1 medium brown onion (150g), sliced thinly
50g snow peas, trimmed
1 medium red capsicum (200g), seeded,
   chopped coarsely
4 green onions, chopped finely

DIPPING SAUCE
1/2 cup (125ml) japanese soy sauce
1 tablespoon mirin
1 tablespoon brown sugar
1 tablespoon grated fresh ginger
1/2 teaspoon sesame oil

1 Shell and devein prawns, leaving tails intact. Combine garlic, sauce and chilli in medium bowl, add prawns, chicken and beef, mix well; stand 15 minutes.

2 Remove and discard mushroom stems; cut a cross in the top of caps.

3 Cook ingredients, except green onions, in batches, on heated oiled grill plate (or grill or barbecue) until vegetables are just tender, prawns and beef are cooked as desired and chicken is cooked through.

4 Serve with green onion and individual bowls of dipping sauce.

   dipping sauce Combine ingredients in medium saucepan; cook, stirring, until sugar dissolves.

   SERVES 4

Adding more ingredients
to the grill plate

vegetables
& salads

simmered green beans

PREPARATION TIME 5 MINUTES · • COOKING TIME 5 MINUTES

Combining ingredients in medium saucepan

Arranging beans in pyramids

Bonito is an oily fish which, when dried and flaked, is widely used in the Japanese kitchen. You could serve the beans with japanese mustard instead of the bonito and use dry white wine instead of sake.

250g green beans, trimmed, cut into 5cm lengths
1¹/₂ cups (375ml) primary dashi (see page 117)
2 tablespoons japanese soy sauce
2 tablespoons sake
2 teaspoons smoked dried bonito flakes (katsuobushi)

1 Combine beans, dashi, sauce and sake in medium saucepan; cover, bring to a boil. Reduce heat, simmer until beans are just tender. Drain beans over small bowl, reserve liquid.

2 Arrange beans in pyramid shapes in individual bowls; pour a little of the reserved cooking liquid over top. Sprinkle with bonito flakes and serve either hot, at room temperature, or chilled.

SERVES 4

tip This dish will keep for two to three days in the refrigerator.

spinach with roasted sesame seed dressing

PREPARATION TIME 5 MINUTES • COOKING TIME 15 MINUTES

Toasting sesame seeds in
small frying pan

Rolling spinach in bamboo mat
to remove excess moisture

*Beans or watercress can be used instead of spinach in this
salad, and peanuts or macadamia nuts could be substituted
for the sesame seeds. If desired, you can garnish the cooked
spinach with katsuobushi (smoked dried bonito flakes).*

$1/3$ cup (50g) white sesame seeds
1 teaspoon sugar
$1^1/2$ tablespoons japanese soy sauce
$1/4$ cup (60ml) primary dashi (see page 117)
600g spinach, trimmed

1 Toast seeds in a heated dry small frying pan, stirring
   constantly. When seeds brown lightly and begin to pop,
   remove from heat. Reserve 1 teaspoon of seeds; blend,
   process or grind remaining hot seeds until smooth.
   Combine ground seeds with sugar, sauce and dashi in
   a screw-top jar; shake well until sugar dissolves.

2 Wash spinach well. Bring medium saucepan of water
   to a boil and immerse spinach for 30 seconds; drain
   immediately. Rinse under cold running water to stop
   cooking and retain colour. Wrap spinach leaves in a
   bamboo mat, roll firmly and gently squeeze out excess
   water; place on serving plate.

3 Just before serving, pour dressing over spinach. Serve at
   room temperature, sprinkled with reserved sesame seeds.

SERVES 4

tip You could use tahini (sesame seed paste) instead
of grinding the toasted sesame seeds.

sweet soy pumpkin

PREPARATION TIME 10 MINUTES • COOKING TIME 15 MINUTES (plus cooling time)

Slicing pumpkin skin to give
a mottled appearance

Turning pumpkin over
during cooking

You will need half a small jap pumpkin to make this recipe.

500g pumpkin, unpeeled
1¹/₂ cups (375ml) secondary dashi (see page 117)
1¹/₂ tablespoons sugar
2 tablespoons mirin
1 tablespoon japanese soy sauce

1 Cut pumpkin into 5cm pieces, discarding seeds. Slice
   skin off at random to give surface a mottled appearance
   and to allow flavour of broth to be absorbed.

2 Place pumpkin in medium saucepan, skin-side down;
   add dashi, sugar and mirin. Bring to a boil; reduce heat,
   simmer, covered, 5 minutes, turning pumpkin pieces
   over after 2 minutes.

3 Add sauce; cook 8 minutes or until pumpkin is tender,
   turning pieces over halfway through cooking time. Remove
   from heat; allow to cool in liquid for a few minutes
   before dividing among individual serving bowls. Serve
   hot or at room temperature with some of the liquid.

SERVES 4

tip You could add stir-fried minced pork or chicken
to pumpkin for a more substantial dish.

five-coloured salad

PREPARATION TIME 20 MINUTES (plus soaking time) • COOKING TIME 10 MINUTES

Soaking mushrooms in
heatproof bowl

Using weight to press tofu
between two boards

Stirring tahini into pureed tofu

6 dried shiitake mushrooms
6cm-long 5cm-diameter piece daikon (120g),
   peeled, sliced thinly lengthways
1 medium carrot (120g), sliced thinly lengthways
115g green beans, quartered lengthways,
   cut into 4cm lengths
8 dried apricots, sliced thinly
1 teaspoon finely shredded lemon rind

DRESSING
200g firm tofu
2 tablespoons tahini
2 teaspoons sugar
2 teaspoons japanese soy sauce
1 tablespoon rice vinegar
1 tablespoon mirin

1 Place mushrooms in small heatproof bowl, cover with
boiling water, stand 20 minutes or until just tender;
drain. Remove and discard stems, slice caps thinly.

2 Boil, steam or microwave daikon, carrot and beans,
separately, until just tender; drain. Rinse under cold
water to cool; drain.

3 Combine apricot and vegetables in medium bowl,
toss gently to combine.

4 Just before serving, pour dressing over salad and mix
through. Divide salad among individual serving bowls,
shape into mounds, sprinkle with rind.

dressing Press tofu between two chopping boards
with a weight on top, raise one end; stand 25 minutes.
Blend or process tofu until smooth, place in small
bowl; stir in tahini. Add remaining ingredients; stir
until sugar dissolves.

SERVES 4

tip The salad and dressing can be prepared ahead and
refrigerated separately. Combine just before serving.

108

daikon and carrot salad

PREPARATION TIME 15 MINUTES (plus soaking time)

Shredding daikon and carrot
on a mandoline

Cutting rolled japanese
mint (shiso) leaves

*This refreshing salad is a perfect accompaniment to barbecued
meat or fish. Shiso (or the beefsteak plant) is a member of
the mint family, and its green leaves lend mint and basil
overtones to this combination. You will need a small daikon
weighing about 400g to make this recipe.*

1¹/₂ cups (360g) finely shredded daikon
2 medium carrots (240g), halved, shredded finely
4 green japanese mint (shiso) leaves
1 tablespoon finely shredded lemon rind
1 teaspoon black sesame seeds
¹/₃ cup (80ml) sushi vinegar (see page 12)

1 Place daikon and carrot in separate medium bowls, cover
  with iced water, stand 15 minutes; drain well.

2 Lay mint leaves on top of each other and roll up;
  cut into thin strips.

3 Combine daikon, carrot and mint in medium bowl;
  sprinkle with rind and seeds. Divide vinegar among
  individual side dishes. Serve salad with vinegar.

SERVES 4

prawn, cucumber and wakame salad

PREPARATION TIME 20 MINUTES (plus standing time)
COOKING TIME 2 MINUTES (plus cooling time)

Scraping seeds from cucumber

Wakame is a highly nutritious seaweed which is dark when dry, but reconstitutes to a bright-green colour. The leaves are usually stripped from the central vein.

1 lebanese cucumber (130g)
1/2 teaspoon salt
4 medium cooked prawns (100g)
10g dried seaweed (wakame)
2cm piece fresh ginger (20g), sliced thinly

DRESSING
1/4 cup (60ml) rice vinegar
11/2 tablespoons primary dashi (see page 117)
11/2 tablespoons japanese soy sauce
3 teaspoons sugar
11/2 tablespoons mirin

Patting salted cucumber dry with absorbent paper

1 Halve cucumber lengthways, scrape out seeds with a spoon and slice finely.

2 Place cucumber in small bowl, sprinkle with salt; stand 15 minutes. Transfer to colander or sieve, rinse under cold water, drain; pat dry with absorbent paper. Shell and devein prawns, halve lengthways. Place in medium bowl with 1 tablespoon of the dressing, stand 10 minutes; add cucumber.

3 Meanwhile, place seaweed in small bowl, cover with cold water; stand 5 minutes or until seaweed softens, drain. Add seaweed to bowl with cucumber, prawns, ginger and remaining dressing; mix gently. Divide among individual serving bowls.

Soaking seaweed in water

dressing Combine ingredients in small saucepan, bring to a boil. Reduce heat; simmer, stirring, until sugar dissolves. Remove from heat; cool.

SERVES 4

tip You can substitute cooked crab meat for the prawns in this salad.

crab and noodle salad with ginger

PREPARATION TIME 15 MINUTES • COOKING TIME 10 MINUTES

Chopping noodles with scissors

Tossing ingredients to combine

Toast sesame seeds in a heated dry small frying pan, stirring constantly. When seeds brown lightly or begin to pop, remove from heat. Soba are buckwheat noodles.

250g dried soba
1/2 cup (100g) cooked crab meat, flaked
1 cup (50g) snow pea sprouts, trimmed
1/2 cup (40g) bean sprouts
6 green onions, chopped finely
1 tablespoon toasted white sesame seeds
2 teaspoons toasted white sesame seeds, extra
1 green onion, chopped finely, extra
1 tablespoon finely shredded red
   pickled ginger (beni-shoga)

DRESSING
1/3 cup (80ml) vegetable oil
1/3 cup (80ml) rice vinegar
2 teaspoons japanese soy sauce
1 teaspoon sugar
1/2 teaspoon sesame oil

1 Cook noodles in large saucepan of boiling water, uncovered, until just tender; drain. Rinse noodles under cold water to cool; drain. Chop noodles with scissors to make them more manageable.

2 Combine noodles, crab, both sprouts, onion, seeds and dressing in a large bowl; toss to combine. Sprinkle salad with extra seeds; serve extra onion and pickled ginger in individual side dishes.

dressing Combine ingredients in screw-top jar; shake well until sugar dissolves.

SERVES 4

tips You can substitute shredded chicken, sliced pressed tofu or sliced beef for the crab.

You could use cellophane (harusame), or dried wheat (somen) noodles instead of soba.

menu suggestions

- Serve clear and thick soups in bowls with lids, if possible, to trap the aroma and flavour. For traditional meals, miso soup is usually served at the end of the meal with the rice and pickles but, for informal meals, serve it as a first course.
- All dishes can be served at once, with mouthfuls of each eaten at random, or you can serve set courses as you do for your usual meals.
- Dessert is usually fresh fruit, cut in decorative patterns; sorbets, sherbets or green tea ice-cream can also be included.
- Green tea is generally served throughout every meal.

LIGHT LUNCH
Miso soup with pork and green
  beans (page 38)
Fried soba (page 58)
Fresh fruit

LUNCH WITH FRIENDS
Deep-fried tofu in broth (page 68)
Spinach with roasted sesame
  seed dressing (page 104)
Salmon teriyaki (page 84)
Steamed rice
Fresh fruit

MAKE-YOUR-OWN SUPPER
Guests not only serve themselves but participate in the preparation of the meal as well.
Sushi hand-rolls (page 22)
Shabu-shabu (page 92)
Daikon and carrot salad (page 110)
Fruit platter or individual sorbet

FAMILY DINNER
This is a simple, traditional meal served at many Japanese restaurants as a set "meal-deal".
Salmon miso and shiitake soup
  (page 48)
Crumbed pork (page 76)
Steamed rice
Individual small plates of pickles
  including pickled daikon,
  quartered and thinly sliced
Fresh fruit

CLASSIC TEMPURA DINNER
Tempura is better suited to a smaller number of people as it should be eaten as soon as it's cooked.
Sashimi rolls (page 30)
Grilled tofu with sesame and
  spinach miso (page 64)
Vegetable and seafood tempura
  (pages 96 and 98) – allow eight
  to 10 pieces per person
Daikon and carrot salad (page 110)
Steamed rice
Sorbet or ice-cream

make your own dashi

Dashi is the basic stock used in nearly every Japanese dish, from small amounts in dipping sauces to far greater amounts in the broths of the famous one-pot dishes such as shabu-shabu (meat and vegetable one-pot) and sukiyaki. It can be either vegetarian, if made only from dried kelp (konbu) and water, or seafood-based, if made from smoked dried bonito flakes (katsuobushi) and water. The most common dashi is made of a combination of both kelp and bonito.

Of several variations, the two most frequently used recipes are **primary dashi** (ichiban-dashi), for clear soups and dipping sauces, and **secondary dashi** (niban-dashi), for thick soups, miso soups, one-pot dishes and most general cooking.

Instant dashi can be purchased in concentrated liquid or granule form – just add water, adjusting the amount to suit your personal taste and the nature of the dish in which it is to be used.

Leftover dashi can be refrigerated in a sealed container for up to three days or frozen for up to one month, but some of its delicate flavour and aroma will be lost. Freeze in measured amounts, such as 1 cup (250ml), or in ice-cube trays. Stir leftover cooked rice into leftover dashi for a quick and easy soup.

PRIMARY DASHI (ICHIBAN-DASHI)

This light stock, subtly flavoured with dried kelp (konbu) and smoked dried bonito flakes (katsuobushi), is used for clear soups and some dipping sauces. Note that the solid ingredients used here should not be discarded if you intend to make secondary dashi (niban-dashi) as well.

> **15g dried kelp (konbu)**
> **1 litre (4 cups) cold water**
> **15g large smoked dried bonito**
>   **flakes (katsuobushi)**

1 Wipe kelp with a damp cloth; cut into three or four large pieces. Place kelp in large saucepan with the water; cook, uncovered, about 10 minutes or until just about to come to a boil.

2 Remove kelp before the mixture comes to a boil.

3 Allow mixture to come just to a boil then add another $1/4$ cup (60ml) cold water and bonito flakes. Return just to a boil, remove from heat immediately.

4 Allow bonito flakes to just start to settle on bottom of saucepan then strain dashi through muslin-lined sieve into another large saucepan. Reserve bonito flakes and kelp for making secondary dashi.

SECONDARY DASHI (NIBAN-DASHI)

This heavier version of stock is made by simmering the dried kelp (konbu) and smoked dried bonito flakes (katsuobushi) used to make primary dashi (ichiban-dashi). It is used for thick and miso soups, seasoned stocks and simmered dishes, where a stronger flavour is required.

> **smoked dried bonito flakes**
>   **(katsuobushi) and dried kelp**
>   **(konbu), reserved from**
>   **primary dashi**
> **1.5 litres (6 cups) cold water**
> **10g smoked dried bonito flakes**
>   **(katsuobushi), extra**

1 Place reserved bonito flakes and kelp in large saucepan with the water; cook, uncovered, about 10 minutes or until just about to come a boil. Reduce heat; simmer, uncovered, about 15 minutes or until dashi reduces by about half.

2 Add extra bonito flakes to pan; remove from heat. Allow bonito flakes to just start to settle on bottom of saucepan then strain dashi through muslin-lined sieve into another large saucepan. bonito flakes and kelp.

INSTANT DASHI

To make light stock (the equivalent of primary dashi) using instant dashi, place $1 1/4$ to $1 1/2$ teaspoons dashi granules (dashi-no-moto) in 1 litre (4 cups) warm water, stirring until dissolved.

To make heavy stock (the equivalent of secondary dashi) using instant dashi, place $1 3/4$ to 2 teaspoons dashi granules (dashi-no-moto) in 1 litre (4 cups) warm water, stirring until dissolved.

index

facts and figures

Wherever you live, you'll be able to use our recipes with the help of these easy-to-follow conversions. While these conversions are approximate only, the difference between an exact and the approximate conversion of various liquid and dry measures is but minimal and will not affect your cooking results.

dry measures

metric	imperial
15g	1/2oz
30g	1oz
60g	2oz
90g	3oz
125g	4oz (1/4lb)
155g	5oz
185g	6oz
220g	7oz
250g	8oz (1/2lb)
280g	9oz
315g	10oz
345g	11oz
375g	12oz (3/4lb)
410g	13oz
440g	14oz
470g	15oz
500g	16oz (1lb)
750g	24oz (1 1/2lb)
1kg	32oz (2lb)

liquid measures

metric	imperial
30ml	1 fluid oz
60ml	2 fluid oz
100ml	3 fluid oz
125ml	4 fluid oz
150ml	5 fluid oz (1/4 pint/1 gill)
190ml	6 fluid oz
250ml	8 fluid oz
300ml	10 fluid oz (1/2 pint)
500ml	16 fluid oz
600ml	20 fluid oz (1 pint)
1000ml (1 litre)	1 3/4 pints

helpful measures

metric	imperial
3mm	1/8in
6mm	1/4in
1cm	1/2in
2cm	3/4in
2.5cm	1in
5cm	2in
6cm	2 1/2in
8cm	3in
10cm	4in
13cm	5in
15cm	6in
18cm	7in
20cm	8in
23cm	9in
25cm	10in
28cm	11in
30cm	12in (1ft)

measuring equipment

The difference between one country's measuring cups and another's is, at most, within a 2 or 3 teaspoon variance. (For the record, 1 Australian metric measuring cup holds approximately 250ml.) The most accurate way of measuring dry ingredients is to weigh them. When measuring liquids, use a clear glass or plastic jug with the metric markings. (One Australian metric tablespoon holds 20ml; one Australian metric teaspoon holds 5ml.)

If you would like to purchase *The Australian Women's Weekly* Test Kitchen's metric measuring cups and spoons (as approved by Standards Australia), turn to page 120 for details and order coupon. You will receive:

- a graduated set of 4 cups for measuring dry ingredients, with sizes marked on the cups.
- a graduated set of 4 spoons for measuring dry and liquid ingredients, with amounts marked on the spoons.

Note: North America, NZ and the UK use 15ml tablespoons. All cup and spoon measurements are level.

We use large eggs having an average weight of 60g.

oven temperatures

These oven temperatures are only a guide. Always check the manufacturer's manual.

	°C (Celsius)	°F (Fahrenheit)	Gas Mark
Very slow	120	250	1
Slow	150	300	2
Moderately slow	160	325	3
Moderate	180 - 190	350 - 375	4
Moderately hot	200 - 210	400 - 425	5
Hot	220 - 230	450 - 475	6
Very hot	240 - 250	500 - 525	7

how to measure

When using graduated metric measuring cups, shake dry ingredients loosely into the appropriate cup. Do not tap the cup on a bench or tightly pack the ingredients unless directed to do so. Level top of measuring cups and measuring spoons with a knife. When measuring liquids, place a clear glass or plastic jug with metric markings on a flat surface to check accuracy at eye level.

Looking after **your interest...**

Keep your Home Library cookbooks clean, tidy and within easy reach with
slipcovers designed to hold up to 12 books. *Plus* you can follow our recipes
perfectly with a set of accurate measuring cups and spoons, as used by
The Australian Women's Weekly Test Kitchen.

To order

Mail or fax Photocopy and complete the
coupon below and post to AWW Home Library
Reader Offer, ACP Direct, PO Box 7036,
Sydney NSW 1028, or fax to (02) 9267 4363.

Phone Have your credit card details
ready, then, if you live in Sydney,
phone 9260 0000; if you live elsewhere
in Australia, phone 1800 252 515
(free call, Mon-Fri, 8.30am-5.30pm).

Price

Book Holder
Australia: $13.10 (incl. GST).
Elsewhere: $A21.95.

Metric Measuring Set
Australia: $6.50 (incl. GST).
New Zealand: $A8.00.
Elsewhere: $A9.95.
Prices include postage and handling.
This offer is available in all countries.

Payment

Australian residents We accept the
credit cards listed on the coupon, money
orders and cheques.

Overseas residents We accept the
credit cards listed on the coupon, drafts
in $A drawn on an Australian
bank, and also British,
New Zealand and U.S.
cheques in the currency of
the country of issue. Credit card
charges are at the exchange rate
current at the time of payment.

Photocopy and complete the coupon below

❑ **Book Holder**

❑ **Metric Measuring Set**
Please indicate number(s) required.

Mr/Mrs/Ms_____

Address_____

_____

Postcode _____ Country _____

Ph: Bus. Hours:(   ) _____

I enclose my cheque/money order for $ _____
payable to ACP Direct

OR: please charge my

❑ Bankcard   ❑ Visa   ❑ MasterCard

❑ Diners Club   ❑ Amex

Card number

Expiry date ____/____

Cardholder's signature _____

Please allow up to 30 days for delivery within Australia.
Allow up to 6 weeks for overseas deliveries.
Both offers expire 31/12/03.   HLJAPCC02

Designer *Caryl Wiggins*
Chief sub-editor *Julie Collard*
Test Kitchen Staff
Food editor *Pamela Clark*
Associate food editor *Karen Hammial*
Assistant food editors *Kirsty McKenzie,
Louise Patniotis*
Test kitchen manager *Elizabeth Hooper*
Home economists *Emma Braz,
Kimberley Coverdale, Kelly Cruickshanks,
Sarah Hine, Sarah Hobbs, Alison Webb*
Editorial coordinator *Juliet Ingersoll*
In-house photographer *Robert Taylor*
In-house stylist *Clare Bradford*
Home Library Staff
Editorial director *Susan Tomnay*
Creative director *Hieu Chi Nguyen*
Senior writer and editor *Lynda Wilton*
Senior editor *Julie Collard*
Designers *Mary Keep, Caryl Wiggins,
Alison Windmill*
Studio manager *Caryl Wiggins*
Editorial coordinator *Holly van Oyen*
Editorial assistant *Lana Meldrum*
Publishing manager (sales) *Jennifer McDonald*
Publishing manager (rights and new projects)
Jane Hazell
Brand manager *Donna Gianniotis*
Pre-press *Harry Palmer*
Production manager *Carol Currie*
Business manager *Sally Lees*
Chief executive officer *John Alexander*
Group publisher *Jill Baker*
Publisher *Sue Wannan*

Produced by ACP Books, Sydney
Printed by Dai Nippon Printing in Korea.
Published by ACP Publishing Pty Limited,
54 Park St, Sydney; GPO Box 4088,
Sydney, NSW 1028.
Ph: (02) 9282 8618 Fax: (02) 9267 9438.
acpbooks@acp.com.au
www.acpbooks.com.au
AUSTRALIA: Distributed by Network Services,
GPO Box 4088,
Sydney, NSW 1028.
Ph: (02) 9282 8777 Fax: (02) 9264 3278.
UNITED KINGDOM: Distributed by Australian
Consolidated Press (UK), Moulton Park
Business Centre, Red House Rd, Moulton Park
Northampton, NN3 6AQ Ph: (01604) 497 531
Fax: (01604) 497 533 acpukltd@aol.com
CANADA: Distributed by Whitecap Books Ltd,
351 Lynn Ave, North Vancouver, BC, V7J 2C4,
Ph: (604) 980 9852 Fax: (604) 980 8197.
customerservice@whitecap.com.ca
www.whitecap.ca
NEW ZEALAND: Distributed by Netlink
Distribution Company, Level 4, 23 Hargreaves St,
College Hill, Auckland 1, Ph: (9) 302 7616.

Cooking class Japanese: step-by-step
to perfect results
Includes index.
ISBN 1 86396 187 9
1. Cookery, Japanese.
(Series: Australian Women's Weekly
Cooking Class).
641.5952
© ACP Publishing Pty Limited 2001
ABN 18 053 273 546
This publication is copyright. No part of it may
be reproduced or transmitted in any form
without the written permission of the publishers.
First published 2001.
Reprinted 2002.
The publishers would like to thank the
following for props used in photography:
Empire Homewares; Lex Dickson Ceramics;
Made in Japan; and Oishi Interiors.